Animal Cruelty

Animal Cruelty

Pathway to Violence against People

Linda Merz-Perez and Kathleen M. Heide

A Division of
ROWMAN & LITTLEFIELD PUBLISHERS, INC.
Lanham • New York • Toronto • Oxford

ALTAMIRA PRESS
A division of Rowman & Littlefield Publishers, Inc.
A wholly owned subsidiary of The Rowman & Littlefield Publishing Group, Inc.
4501 Forbes Boulevard, Suite 200
Lanham, MD 20706
www.altamirapress.com

PO Box 317
Oxford
OX2 9RU, UK

British Library Cataloguing in Publication Information Available

Library of Congress Cataloging-in-Publication Data

Merz-Perez, Linda, 1954–
  Animal Cruelty: Pathway to Violence against People / Linda Merz-Perez
and Kathleen M. Heide.
    p. cm.
Includes bibliographical references and index.
  ISBN 0-7591-0303-8 (alk. paper)—ISBN 0-7591-0304-6 (pbk.: alk.
paper)
  1. Animal welfare—Psychological aspects. 2. Cruelty. 3. Violence in
children. 4. Conduct disorders in children. 5. Criminal behavior,
Prediction of. I. Heide, Kathleen M., 1954– II. Title.

  HV4708.M47 2003
  364.1'87—dc21

                                                        2003011613

Printed in the United States of America

To my mother, Barbara Merz, and to the memory of my father, Bill Merz, and grandmother, Julia Hall ("Mamie"), whose love provided me the gift of a childhood framed by tolerance, trust, and laughter, in which "fear" was a word unknown; to my husband, Ignacio Perez, whose understanding of my work empowered me to follow my heart; to my brother, Bill, whose compassion served to enhance my own; and to the memory of my beloved Andrew, the dog who opened my eyes to the world of animal sheltering and taught me to be a voice for the voiceless.

Linda Merz-Perez

To my mother, Eleanor Heide-Halligan, and to my brother, Thomas Robert Heide, two people whose lives exemplify strength tempered with compassion, love, and gentleness; a solid sense of values; and a great sense of humor—qualities that have enriched the lives of all who know them.

Kathleen M. Heide

CONTENTS

PART FOUR
A BLUEPRINT TO END SENSELESS PAIN AND DESTRUCTION

FOREWORD

I recently had the opportunity to view two sets of home movies. In the first, a cute blond boy of about five wanders a bit unsteadily in a large yard, smiling broadly as he carries a toy gun. A cat comes and rubs affectionately against his legs as the boy walks toward the camera. At the end of the scene, the boy's mother lifts him up to her shoulders and carries him off, smiling. In the second film, a cute blond boy about five years old walks a bit awkwardly carrying two sparklers. His smile is bright and cheerful. A dog enters the scene and gives the boy a friendly sniff. At the end of the film, the boy's father lifts him to his shoulders and carries him off, smiling. Both films are unremarkable, reminiscent of hundreds of home movies taken by parents of baby-boom children. However, both movies are particularly meaningful for me. The first film is from my own childhood, and the boy with the gun is me. The little boy in the second film is Jeffrey Dahmer.

One of the greatest challenges to those of us concerned about crime and violence is that there are so many potential forces at work that can lead an individual down many different paths. It is often tempting to simply dismiss individuals like Jeffrey Dahmer as being alien, totally different from the rest of us, freaks of nature and nurture warped by chaotic, violent childhoods into monsters that prey upon us from the shadows. My own experiences with such offenders are echoed by the case histories described in this volume. Most prisoners, even the most violent ones, are more like us than different from us. Although their deeds may be monstrous, they are rarely the monsters depicted in popular fiction. What is often fascinating and disturbing is their ordinariness, at least in childhood, and their similarity to ourselves and the people we know.

Although many of our most violent offenders came from backgrounds of chaos and abuse, others emerged from families that were disturbingly like our own. Although most perpetrators of extreme violence were victims of, or witnesses to, violence in the home, most people with such histories do not become perpetrators, and many of the resilient survivors of violent families enter into helping and healing professions. Students of antisocial and criminal behavior, including the authors of this volume, have realized that violent behavior is like a complex ecosystem with many interwoven connections. Some components may have a greater overall influence on the health of the whole system, but everything is potentially connected to everything else. Just as ecologists look at the condition of "sentinel" species, such as frogs or birds of prey, to alert them to dangers that threaten the ecosystem, criminologists seek to find certain sentinel behaviors that may provide the early warning that something is amiss in an individual's adjustment to society. They are looking for the "red flag" that provides a reliable indicator that we need to be concerned about the path a person is traveling.

Linda Merz-Perez and Kathleen Heide have chosen to focus on one such set of behaviors, namely, cruelty to animals. They bring unique credentials to this examination. Merz-Perez, in addition to her criminal justice training, has served as a guardian *ad litem*, looking after the interests of abused and neglected children. She has also served as the director of several humane societies. Heide, a professor of criminology at a major research university and a licensed mental health professional, has a distinguished career looking at the dynamics of violence in many violent offenders. Their collaboration has brought an original orientation to these issues that has combined careful attention to quantitative method and strongly held concern for the victims of violence, regardless of their species. They provide a careful and cogent assessment of past research in this field, and fresh results from carefully crafted interviews.

The notion that people who are intentionally and repeatedly cruel to animals are at risk of violence against people has been part of our popular culture for centuries. One of the oldest representations of this is the traditional Punch and Judy show. Although the story has become sanitized over the years, from its origins in the Middle Ages through its peak in the nineteenth century, the fable was one of the archetypal escalation of violence. Twitchell (1989) presents a reconstruction of the traditional morality play from an 1827 performance. In it, Punch calls for his wife Judy, but Toby, the neighbor's dog comes instead. Punch bludgeons the dog, then beheads the neighbor. When his child soils himself, Punch beats the child's head on the stage and throws him into the audience. He then pummels Judy to death, and, as the story develops, he proceeds to kill a doctor, a servant, a policeman, and the hangman. Finally Punch must confront the Devil himself, and he succeeds in impaling the Devil on his own pitchfork! This theme has been repeated many times in art, literature, and film. Virtually every American born in the twentieth century learned a lesson in the connections between animal abuse and human violence when, in the film *The Wizard of Oz*, they heard the Wicked Witch of the West threaten Dorothy and Toto with the unforgettable threat "I'll get you . . . and your little dog too."

Ironically, scientific attempts to confirm the widely held belief in this connection were slow in coming. Merz-Perez and Heide provide a good historical review of the efforts of Felthous, Kellert, and others to clarify this connection, and they provide a clear analysis of some studies that, for a variety of reasons, failed to find such a connection.

This report is rich in insights into the lives of men who have taken a turn in the wrong direction and raises some new concerns. Many of these men, as we would have expected, had early histories of cruelty to animals. Less expected, but particularly disturbing to me, is the large number of men in this study who had witnessed acts of serious violence against animals and did or felt nothing. This may be, unfortunately, an increasingly common phenomenon. I routinely hear teachers and humane educators voice concern that many of the elementary school children they speak with have witnessed or even participated in dogfighting or other acts of cruelty. Such "street" fighting has become a major concern for local and national humane groups, which see this as a problem that brings the connections between guns, drugs, gangs, and animal abuse into the heart of many of our cities. The authors point out the need to empower those who witness such acts to take action to stop them or prevent their recurrence and to reexamine the societal and cultural norms that continue to allow people to dismiss such aberrant behavior as insignificant.

Ultimately this work, like other important research that preceded it, is aimed at better understanding one of the greatest questions we face: the nature and origins of evil. Whether violence against animals, children, women, and others is a pathological or a purposeful act, what are the factors that allow or encourage such acts to take place? Popular culture once again suggests some answers. Brian Cox, the first actor to portray serial killer Hannibal Lecter, in the 1986 film *Manhunter*, described his method of trying to grasp the behavior of someone capable of engaging in such hideous acts while still being able to function at a very high level. He notes that he drew his inspiration for his portrayal of a brilliant murderer from a remark made by one of the judges at the Nuremberg trials of Nazi war criminals. The judge believed that "evil is the absence of empathy." Clearly many of the violent men interviewed for this study are without empathy for other living things, human or nonhuman. Others may have some empathy and are able to perceive the mental and emotional state of their victims, but they are without the sympathy to care. Finally, the most dangerous are those who lack empathy and sympathy and whose behavior is guided by a narcissistic sense of entitlement to avenge the real or imagined injustices that life has presented to them.

Rarely do such problems arise without warning, but the warnings may be unheeded if the victim is "only an animal." Merz-Perez and Heide have given us a new and stronger reason to take animal abuse very seriously.

—Randall Lockwood, Ph.D.

ACKNOWLEDGMENTS

We wish to express our deep appreciation to the colleagues, professional associates, and friends who contributed to this book. We especially thank Randall Lockwood, Ph.D., vice president of research and educational outreach, the Humane Society of the United States, Washington, D.C. and Frank R. Ascione, Ph.D., professor, Department of Psychology, Utah State University, for their ongoing dedication to this project. They have made many contributions to the field of animal cruelty and to the present research. We are honored that Dr. Lockwood provided the foreword to our book and that Dr. Ascione completed our work with his afterword.

We also wish to thank the Florida Department of Corrections for approving the study that made this book possible. We are grateful to institutional staff at the maximum security facility for their cooperation and assistance in conducting our research.

We are grateful to our editor, Rosalie Robertson of AltaMira Press, for her editorial assistance and enthusiasm for this project from its conception to its completion. We appreciate the excellent copyediting of Cheryl Hoffman and all of the assistance of Lori Pierelli, production editor, and Kristina van Niekerk, editorial assistant, throughout the production process. We would like to acknowledge Denise Paquette Boots, M.A., doctoral candidate at the University of South Florida (USF), and Mary Kay Hartung, M.A., research librarian, for helping us keep on top of the latest literature on animal cruelty. Special thanks to Mary Sweely, executive secretary to Dr. Heide, who graciously did "all the little things that go along with a big project." We are indebted to Eldra P. Solomon, Ph.D., who reviewed select portions of this manuscript and made excellent editorial suggestions.

ACKNOWLEDGMENTS

Linda Merz-Perez wishes to thank the Department of Criminology, University of South Florida, for supporting her professional and intellectual endeavors. She is particularly grateful to Dr. Ira J. Silverman for the avid interest he displayed years ago with respect to her graduate studies. She is also grateful to the many organizations that have supported her work on behalf of animals and children, in both Florida and Alabama: the SPCA of West Pasco, Pasco County Animal Control, the West Pasco Bar Association, Florida Voices for Animals, the State of Florida Guardian Ad Litem Program, Shelby Humane Society, and Hand-in-Paw.

Kathleen M. Heide would like to thank Renu Khator, dean of the College of Arts and Sciences, University of South Florida, for the opportunity to complete this manuscript while serving as associate dean. She extends her gratitude to all the staff in the dean's office who made sure that she was well fed and had lots of laughs to make it through the day. Dr. Heide acknowledges with great appreciation the support and friendship of USF Provost David Stamps and Dwayne Smith, chair of criminology. Kathleen would also like to thank her friends and Mastermind partners— Fran, Donna, Barnie, Marsha, Lisa, Jack, and Gina—for seeing this book through to completion.

Part One
ANIMAL CRUELTY:
THE CURRENT STATE OF KNOWLEDGE

CHAPTER ONE
ANIMAL CRUELTY ENCAPSULATED

Acts of animal cruelty happen countless times a day across the United States and around the world. Particularly heinous acts are often headlined in newspapers and profiled on the evening news. Readers and viewers alike typically recoil with horror. When children are identified as the perpetrators, the public often asks, "What's next?" Concern focuses on whether animal cruelty is a pathway to later violence directed against humans. This book examines the evidence linking cruelty to animals with violence against people.

Although animal cruelty seems like a simple concept, it is a complex phenomenon. Animal cruelty manifests itself in many ways and is fueled by many motives. Some incidents are intentional and involve acts of overt cruelty. In other instances, the cruelty is passive and is termed neglect. The following four examples are not to be read by the squeamish. They are real-life cases of animal cruelty and illustrate the many forms that it can take.

In the first case, the animal, a black chow, approximately one year of age, was brought to the shelter by a municipal animal control agency. Staff reported that the animal could not stand on its own and needed to be lifted from the back of the truck. The animal was to be euthanized but died as soon as it was removed from the truck. Staff requested the presence of the senior author to examine the animal. The animal had a gunshot entry wound on the top of the head. Upon closer observation, it became apparent that the left side of the animal's face had been bashed in with a blunt instrument of some kind. Some of the animal's teeth had been completely knocked out, while others hung by a thread from the animal's bloody jaw. The animal control officers claimed that they had no knowledge of how the animal came to be in this condition. The young chow was one example of the anonymous and tragic fate met by so many animals.

In another instance, a passerby came to the shelter to report that an animal, apparently a beagle mix, was lying in a small field adjacent to the shelter property. The animal was whimpering. The senior author went to the scene with two staff members. The animal had about three feet of rope around its neck. Upon examining the animal, it was clear that the animal had been dragged behind a vehicle. The pads of the animal's feet were completely rubbed away by road burn, and they were raw and bloody. The animal's chest was bleeding, and the skin was torn away in several places. Gravel was embedded in the wounds, adding to the animal's suffering. The staff's first instinct was to euthanatize the animal, but the animal looked at us with such intensity that we carefully lifted her and rushed her to a local veterinarian. After a series of skin grafts, sutures, meticulous applications of various medications, soothing baths, and bandage changes, the young dog recuperated and was ultimately adopted. We named her Slippers because we covered her bandaged feet with little pink waterproof "doggie slippers" to keep the bandages clean and dry. Once again, the cruelty that Slippers sustained was anonymously perpetrated.

Another instance of cruelty involved a collie mix that came to be named Tripod. The animal was brought to the shelter after losing one leg, supposedly by being driven over by accident by the neighbor's car. The remaining stub, however, appeared to be the product of a clean slice, such as could have been made with a meat cleaver. The animal, which was immediately given veterinary care, survived. During the treatment period, a neighbor of the owner contacted the shelter and related that the owner's boyfriend had indeed chopped off the animal's leg during a violent argument with the owner. The neighbor refused to provide further information or to come forward. She was afraid of the owner's boyfriend, who drank and was violent. Once again, an animal suffered anonymously. Because of caring human intervention provided by the shelter and the veterinarian, the animal was saved and ultimately adopted. Furthermore, the animal has compensated for her missing leg just fine. She is now living in a home where she is a loved and cherished member of the family.

A cruelty case that was successfully prosecuted involved a six-month-old chow puppy that had to be euthanatized as a result of extreme neglect. The case came to the shelter as a result of complaints from several people. The animal was infested with advanced sarcoptic mange, which had caused both internal and external secondary bacterial infections. The animal was nearly hairless, and the skin had the texture and color of an elephant's hide. The top of the animal's head looked like a skull in that the skin had thickened and calcified. Pus exuded from the animal's eyes, and it had difficulty standing upon our arrival on the scene. The animal was extremely malnourished, and the skeletal frame was clearly visible beneath the hairless skin. The animal's nails had been permitted to grow so long that they curled around and had begun to grow into the animal's footpads. The man who was convicted neither demonstrated remorse nor accepted responsibility for the animal's pitiful condition.

Millions of animals each year in the United States alone become victims of cruelty and neglect. In many instances, animal cruelty is concealed by anonymity. It takes courage for witnesses to come forward. In many cases, the abuser is described as a dangerous or violent person. Therefore, law enforcement must play a proactive and supportive role in assisting people who are willing to come forward and in guiding cruelty cases through the court system. Ultimately, animal cruelty can be faced head-on as a *crime* only when all concerned embrace the perception that animals can indeed be *victims.*

This study was designed to explore the relationship between cruelty to animals and later violence directed against humans. Emphasis was placed on violent offenders in an effort to determine whether the phenomenon of cruelty to animals might serve as an early warning sign of predictable future violence against humans. Previous research investigating the role of animal cruelty as a precursor to violence has resulted in inconsistent findings. Debate has focused in particular on whether animal cruelty should be viewed as an entity in and of itself or as part of a constellation of factors associated with subsequent violence by adults. Furthermore, the issue persists as to the status of cruelty to animals with respect to its being a crime. It is only in recent years that animals are indeed being viewed as potential victims. In addition, the term *cruelty to animals* is a highly generalized one that must be analyzed within the context of diverse cultural and individual standards of interpretation and significance. This study draws attention to some of the inconsistencies in previous research that have been perpetuated in the literature.

This chapter provides an overview of the two landmark studies that initiated inquiry into the phenomenon of cruelty to animals as a factor related to human violence. To understand the context of this study, it is helpful to know the history behind the development of animal cruelty laws. After a brief discussion of the laws from a historical perspective, we examine the evolution of definitions of animal cruelty. We then look at how animal cruelty is affected by varying cultural ramifications. The chapter concludes by addressing the compelling reasons for further study of the phenomenon of cruelty to animals and its relationship to human violence.

Beginning in the 1960s, research with respect to cruelty to animals most often examined the phenomenon as part of the *triad,* a set of behaviors suspected of being associated with manifestations of aggression. MacDonald (1963) and Hellman and Blackman (1966) were the pioneering figures in the emerging field of study focusing on animal cruelty.

Pioneers of the Triad

MacDonald was a pioneering figure in the debate on the role of animal cruelty as a predictive factor. In a study involving hospitalized patients, MacDonald (1963), a psychiatrist, focused on patients who had threatened to kill rather than on patients who had killed, although some of the subjects later committed homicide. His sample consisted of forty-eight psychotic and fifty-two nonpsychotic patients. He found that very sadistic patients often had three characteristics in common in their childhood histories. These factors, which became known as the *MacDonald Triad,* consisted of bedwetting (enuresis), firesetting, and torturing small animals. MacDonald's study targeted the core issue of whether the triad could be used as a preemptive tool to intervene and possibly circumvent violent behavior. The psychiatrist argued that the triad was a superior predictor to paranoid delusions because many patients with violent paranoid delusions do not kill. MacDonald concluded, as a result of prior studies that focused on homicidal subjects, that a history of great parental brutality, extreme maternal seduction, and the triad was a likely prognostic factor of future homicidal behavior. He also concluded that the triad was an unfavorable prognostic factor in those who had threatened, but had not committed, homicide. Therefore, according to MacDonald, the appearance of the triad was of little value as a potential barometer of future homicidal behavior.

Contrary to MacDonald, the psychiatrists Hellman and Blackman (1966) endorsed the predictive potential of the triad, concluding that its presence in childhood might be important in predicting violent antisocial behavior. On the basis of their findings, the authors argued that the detection and early management of children in the throes of the triad might well forestall a career of violent crime in adulthood. Hellman and Blackman theorized about the meaning behind enuresis and firesetting. They described enuresis as the unintentional voiding of urine, usually occurring during sleep and persisting in the individual past the age of five years. They argued that enuresis represents a form of sadism or hostility because the act of voiding is equated in fantasy with damaging and destroying. According to these authors, enuresis is intimately related to firesetting.

Their study also supported firesetting as a manifestation of the type of aggression associated with enuresis. Firesetting was defined as "setting particular objects on fire as a child; for example, setting fire to a shed or car, collecting refuse and combustible materials in order to build bonfires, homemade bombs, home flame throwers out of lighter fluid cans and the like" (Hellman & Blackman, 1966, p. 1432). Firesetting had also been found to be an integral trait in Japanese children who show other aggressive acting out and delinquent behavior.

Hellman and Blackman (1966) defined cruelty to animals as the killing or torturing of dogs, cats, pets, or baby animals. The authors considered the torture of dogs and cats to be a more significant indicator of future violent behavior than the torture of such animals as flies, toads, and turtles. Dogs and cats are more humanlike; torturing and killing them violates the human bond with pets. Hellman and Blackman noted that Margaret Mead had observed cruelty to animals in a variety of cultures. Mead suggested that the torturing or killing of what she termed *good animals* (animals deemed worthy of human nurturing and protection, such as a pet animal) by the child might be a precursor to more violent acts as an adult. On the basis of Mead's observations, broad cultural applications of the triad were inferred.

Hellman and Blackman reported that a strong relationship exists between parental loss or rejection and the evolution of personality disorders and mental illness. They maintained that the loss of, or rejection by, a parent causes not only primary separation anxiety but also aggression, whose function is to achieve reunion.

After nearly four decades of study, the triad remains an area of interest. The inconsistencies that have been cited are informative. They do not refute the proposed correlation of cruelty to animals as a predictor of violence directed against humans. Rather, they suggest that the variables examined to date have been too generalized and that the correlation itself has problems of verification. In this study, the term *correlation* always refers to the specific phenomenon of cruelty to (or toward) animals and violence against human beings. The term *triad* always refers to the three components as specified by such researchers as Hellman and Blackman, with one of the three being cruelty to animals.

Cruelty To Animals: A Historical Perspective

The nineteenth century brought about a transformation in animal cruelty laws (Favre & Tsang, 1993). This transformation ultimately resulted in the recognition that an animal's potential for pain and suffering was real and animals deserved protection against its unnecessary infliction. This recognition was indeed an evolutionary process. In Great Britain, Rev. Humphrey Primatt in *A Dissertation on the Duty of Mercy and Sin of Cruelty to Brute Animals*, written in 1776, pleaded for the compassionate treatment of animals: "See that no brute of any kind whether entrusted to thy care, or coming in thy way, suffer thy neglect or abuse" (p. 33). His view was progressive, given that standing laws addressing animal cruelty well into the nineteenth century existed primarily as a remedy for economic loss resulting from the injury or death of an animal that represented the owner's revenue or the means to revenue. In this context, Reverend Humphrey was truly before his time when he added, "Let no views of profit, no compliance with custom, and no fear of ridicule of the world, ever tempt thee to the least act of cruelty or injustice to any creature whatsoever" (p. 33).

Despite Reverend Humphrey's fervent call for compassion, his words did not result in the passage of laws until much later. In the United States, laws were first designed to protect animals for the value they represented as property. The Vermont Criminal Code, LAWS 34, section 34.2, adopted in 1846, provides a good example: "Every person who shall willfully and maliciously kill, wound, maim or disfigure any horse, or horses, or horse kind, cattle, sheep, or swine, of another person, or shall willfully or maliciously administer poison to any such animal . . . shall be punished by imprisonment of . . . not more than five years, or fined not exceeding five hundred dollars" (p. 38).

The fact that a crime was committed only if the animal in question was owned by somebody else is another clear indication that these laws were designed to protect *property*. As early as 1821, however, the germ of a perceptual change appeared in a Maine statute (Maine Laws chap. 4, sec. 7) that used the language "That if any person shall cruelly beat any horse or cattle" (p. 39), there would be legal ramifications. Although this law was extremely narrow in terms of the type of animals it protected and the specific act (beating) from which it protected them, the key word for change was *any*. No distinction was made on the basis of ownership. Very tentatively, the stage was being set for the development of the notion that animals deserve protection in their own right and not merely as property.

The foundation for the animal cruelty statutes that exist today was laid beginning in the 1860s by Henry Bergh of New York. In 1866, Bergh orchestrated a change in the 1829 version of the New York cruelty statute (N.Y. Penal Law 26), which had existed unchanged since its initial passage. As in the case of most laws that were currently operative throughout the various states, the 1829 New York law contained two problems in terms of its ability to protect animals. First, it limited the types of animals protected to animals associated with revenue (horses, mules, oxen, cattle, sheep); and, second, it required that the abuser be someone other than the owner (Favre & Tsang, 1993). The implication was clear. If an owned animal was property, then the owner could do with it as he pleased because the property had no rights of its own.

It was these two issues that Berg successfully addressed in what came to be the revised, 1866 version of the law. First, the language was changed to include the words "any other animal" (and not just the animals previously cited). Second, the act of abuse itself was no longer limited to that committed by a person other than the owner; the law now included the words "belonging to himself or another" (p. 45). The two words *any* and *another* initiated a revolutionary change in the conceptual and legal framework within which the United States would eventually begin to recognize animals.

Also in 1866, the New York Legislature granted a charter, sought by Bergh, recognizing the American Society for the Prevention of Cruelty to Animals (ASPCA) statewide. The expressed purpose of the ASPCA was to provide effective means for the prevention of cruelty to animals, to enforce all laws enacted for the protection of animals, and to secure the arrest and conviction of those who violated such laws. In 1888, Bergh was elected as the ASPCA's first president.

The evolution of laws did not end in 1866. Protection of animals remains a difficult affair, complicated by the highly diverse views held by humans toward animals and the cultural parameters within which humans establish the values and practices that affect animals. Culture directly determines the use or abuse of animals and even the very meaning of these words. As a result, the protection of animals from neglect and abuse remains a process and not a finite act resolved by any law. The controversy that was ignited over the issue of religious freedom in the city of Hialeah, Florida, is a case in point. That city's ban on animal sacrifices, as practiced by followers of the Afro-Cuban religion of Santeria, battled its way to the Supreme Court. In 1993, the Supreme Court upheld the right of the followers of Santeria to practice their religion freely, even with respect to animal sacrifice (Billitteri, 1993). The Court's decision did not prohibit, in theory, the appropriate enforcement of Hialeah's anticruelty laws, but it certainly created a gray area that complicates animal protection in practice.

In addition to any constitutional considerations that might affect animal cruelty laws, there remains the elementary issue of enforcement. Clearly, any law that is not enforced is useless, and many cruelty statutes currently on the books are not enforced in practice. The reasons for this situation are varied. In many instances animal cruelty laws are not enforced simply because neither they nor the animals that they are meant to protect are perceived to be important enough. The findings by Vermeulen and Odendaal (1993) support this view. The authors conclude that "the seriousness [of animal cruelty] is often underestimated by the judicial system, the abuser, and society as a whole and not given necessary attention" (p. 399). The authors' frame of reference for their study was South Africa, suggesting, perhaps, that the legal standing of animals worldwide is nebulous.

Lockwood (1999) provides a reflective overview of the factors that have heightened the recognition of the phenomenon of cruelty to animals. Lockwood cites a 1996 survey that indicated a high level of public interest and concern about animal cruelty. For example, 75 percent of survey respondents reported that they would be more likely to support a political candidate who favored tougher animal cruelty laws. Close to a third (32 percent) indicated that tougher laws against animal cruelty should be supported because such behavior was an indication of violence in the home. Furthermore, about 30 percent of the respondents reported that cruelty to animals was simply and inherently wrong and that defenseless animals should not be subjected to such treatment.

Lockwood cited factors that, in his view, contributed to the growing awareness of, and concern with, animal cruelty. These factors included: (a) stronger scientific support for the connection between animal cruelty and violence against humans; (b) overall growth of the animal welfare, animal protection, and animal rights movements; (c) specific campaigns of animal advocacy groups; and (d) societal concern about violence. Lockwood concluded that, although the legal status of animals has remained unchanged since the introduction of animal welfare reforms more than a century ago, the increasing societal awareness of the role of cruelty to animals "in the much broader universe of antisocial and criminal behavior" is "an important step on the path to a truly humane society" (Lockwood, 1999, p. 7).

Cazaux (1999) also provided a historical overview of perceptions toward animals and concludes that a nonspeciesist criminology is needed. Cazaux said that "although interactions between people and other animals play an important part in the social agenda, this topic has been mostly ignored by criminological academics" (p. 105). Cazaux noted that throughout history, both religion and philosophy have delegated animals to the control and caprices of humans. As a point of departure, the author cited the first chapter of Genesis, which urges man to "have dominion over the fish of the sea and over the birds of the air and over every living thing that moves on earth" (p. 107).

This view was mirrored by Jewish and Greek thinkers, noted Cazaux, and this perspective remained fairly constant into the Middle Ages. The emergence of humanism during the Renaissance reinforced the idea that man occupies a unique place in the universe, and by the time of Descartes (seventeenth century), animals were viewed as mere machines. A disruption in this continuum of thinking did not occur until the 1780s, when Jeremy Bentham, in "A Utilitarian View," asserted, "The question is not Can they reason, nor Can they talk, but, Can they suffer?" (cited in Cazaux, 1999, pp. 109–110).

Cazaux followed this modernistic discourse into the twentieth century, citing the development of animal rights perspectives that referred to animals other than humans as "nonhuman animals" (Cazaux, 1999, p. 110).

Singer and Regan focused primarily on the institutionalized use and abuse of animals in such settings as factory farming and biomedical research. Singer defined speciesism as a phenomenon that fosters a biased attitude favoring the interests of one's own species. Cazaux also cited the simultaneously evolving ecofeminist view that proposed that until patriarchal mentality is ended in all its forms, oppression will not end.

Cazaux next examined current approaches to the study of animal cruelty that view animal abuse within the context of its relationship to human violence, citing such researchers as Kellert and Felthous (1985). Cazaux recognized that typologies of cruelty to animals within this context (which supposes a link between animal abuse and other expressions of interpersonal violence) are appropriately gaining greater attention. He noted, however, that many cases of abuse are tied to human attachment and are personalized (i.e., they involve companion animals) and thus represent an anthropocentric view. In this vein, the author argued that billions of animals annually are exploited anonymously by the food, cosmetics, and biomedical industries, a fact ignored by criminological research. Cazaux concluded that the criminological arena must not "ignore these large scale systems of animal abuse." Rather, research must adopt an approach that is nonspeciesist rather than anthropocentric.

Animal Cruelty Defined

Cruelty to animals, as suggested by the above discussion, encompasses varying dimensions. Regional differences in its perception and identification due to cultural factors and varying definitions under law complicate this issue. According to most laws in the United States, failure to provide adequate food, water, and shelter or the use of physical force to leave a mark or otherwise cause injury constitutes cruelty to animals. The penalties under these laws, however, vary greatly from state to state. In Florida, for example, "A person who unnecessarily overloads, overdrives, torments, deprives of necessary sustenance or shelter, or unnecessarily or cruelly beats, mutilates, or kills any animal, or causes the same to be done, or carries in or upon any vehicle, or otherwise, any animal in a cruel or inhumane manner, is guilty of a misdemeanor of the first degree" (Florida State Statute 828.12). The maximum penalty for such an offense is one year in jail or a $5,000 fine, or both.

In 1988, the Florida statutes pertaining to animal abuse were toughened with respect to acts deemed excessively cruel. The case that brought about this change in law involved a Doberman pinscher that was soaked in gasoline and set on fire by two teenaged boys. The judge made an appeal to the legislature that extreme animal cruelty be made a third-degree felony. The state legislature subsequently passed a felony law, which became effective on October 1, 1989, stating that "any person who tortures any animal with intent to inflict intense pain, serious injury, or death upon the animal is guilty of a felony in the third degree" (Florida State Statute 828.12). A third-degree felony carries a maximum penalty of a term of imprisonment not exceeding five years or a fine of not more than $10,000, or both.

Establishing a working definition of cruelty to animals is central to enforcement. Kellert and Felthous (1985) established clear parameters of cruelty to animals that have often been referenced both in research and in practice by those who have attempted to address the phenomenon of cruelty to animals. The authors list various acts as extreme cruelty to animals. These include a wide diversity of behaviors with varying degrees of severity and cultural meaning and implication. Among them were deliberately inflicting pain or torturing a pet animal, similar acts toward wildlife and livestock, prolonging the slaughter of a domestic animal (e.g., inhumane killing of livestock), skinning a trapped animal alive, stoning or beating an animal, exploding an animal, wounding an animal on purpose, entering a dog in a dogfight, throwing an animal off a high place, pulling the wings off animals, tying two animals' tails together, electrocuting an animal, burning an animal, blinding an animal, cutting off parts of an animal, breaking an animal's bones, and pouring chemical irritants on an animal. A number of other behaviors were considered possible indicators of animal cruelty, although the social acceptability of these acts could be linked to particular value standards. These acts include participation in a cockfight, harsh physical punishment during the training of an animal, and sexual play with an animal. The authors note that particular phobias with respect to animals also prompt acts of cruelty.

Historically and up to the present time, research examining the relationship of cruelty to animals and later violence against humans has been complicated by the fact that it is extremely difficult to quantify acts of animal cruelty. To date, a centralized reporting procedure has not been developed to collect and analyze data from the many agencies in the United

States that respond to animal cruelty cases. Police agencies, humane societies, animal control facilities, mental health services, and, in some instances, child investigative and protection services face networking difficulties in their efforts to address animal cruelty. This lack of centralization, in combination with the difficulties of definition, complicates the issue further.

Obviously, procedural and operational changes are required to facilitate centralization and interagency cooperation. Such changes require administrative and organizational remedies that will result in practical solutions. The issue of definition, however, is more conceptual in nature. Animal cruelty cannot be addressed unless those in the field have a clear understanding of what it is.

Kellert and Felthous (1985) significantly contributed to establishing precise definitions of animal cruelty. The authors described nine motives for cruelty to animals (pp. 1122–1124), which are summarized as follows:

1. to control an animal

2. to retaliate against an animal

3. to satisfy a prejudice against a species or breed

4. to express aggression through an animal

5. to enhance one's own aggressiveness

6. to shock people for amusement

7. to retaliate against another person

8. displacement of hostility from a person to an animal

9. nonspecific sadism.

The nine motives presented by Kellert and Felthous provide a conceptual foundation for further research on animal cruelty and for more precise definition and refinement of animal cruelty laws.

Cultural Influences and Animal Cruelty

The recognition of cruelty to animals is complicated by cultural factors. For example, in parts of Latin America and the United States, cockfighting is perceived as a legitimate sport even in areas where it is illegal. It is often said that perception is nine-tenths of the law, and cockfighting is a good example of this adage. The case of Curtis Blackwell is another good example of why cruelty to animals can be conceptually problematic. Upon Blackwell's death, the *Birmingham News* (Gerome, 1999) reviewed the life of the Alabama native who raised and fought roosters for most of his eighty-one years. The article reported that Blackwell learned cockfighting as a young man, at a time when it was considered a "gentleman's sport" (p. 3E). Blackwell's own philosophy about the sport was that "If God didn't want 'em to fight, they wouldn't" (p. 3E). According to the article, many who knew Blackwell thought of him as a "respected landowner who could be warm and engaging in conversation" (p. 3E).

Blackwell personifies the difficulty in both defining and responding to cruelty to animals. According to many, Blackwell was a gentleman who loved his sport and loved his cocks. According to others, including the area humane societies, Blackwell's "sport" was animal cruelty, and according to the law, this cruelty was a criminal act. This conceptual confusion affects how humans deal with animals. Blackwell might have made a compelling argument that, compared to the chickens in factory farming, his cocks lived lives of honor and pride. The egg industry, for example, destroys all male chicks soon after birth, for obvious reasons, and the hens that survive live solely to lay eggs in such crowded conditions that their beaks are trimmed to prevent them from harming one another. Yet, factory farming is both a culturally sanctioned institution and a major financial industry in the United States. Few consider it cruel. Fewer still entertain the thought that it might be cruel.

The contradictory perceptions that culture engenders need not, and should not, impede the study of cruelty to animals and its relationship to human violence. To illustrate this point, it should be reiterated that Mead emphasized that it was the killing of good animals that was relevant to the correlation. Mead described good animals as those that engender human compassion and protection, such as pet animals. This is not to imply that Mead advocated a compartmentalization of human compassion with respect to animals. She did contend, however, that humans who are cruel to good animals clearly betray the standards of behavior that measure and define our very humanity.

Contradiction is a given in human behavior, but when contradictions are properly conceptualized, meaningful understanding about human behavior often emerges. For example, a criminal who murders another human being is incarcerated, while a soldier who kills for his country is celebrated as a hero. Regardless of individual religious or ethical considerations relative to the taking of human life, this qualitative difference can be categorically applied by a society at large to distinguish murder from justified killing. In fact, no society can survive without reconciling the many contradictions posed by human nature.

A similar perceptual process of differentiation and reconciliation can and must be applied to the study of cruelty to animals if any meaningful understanding is to result. The contradictory uses and abuses of animals must be conceptually addressed. It should also be stated here that intellectual reconciliation is a very different process from ethical reconciliation.

Kellert and Felthous (1985) emphasized the importance of identifying motives for animal abuse and of establishing any applicable patterns of abuse as a remedy to the contradictory elements that cultural parameters impart to the study of cruelty to animals. An understanding of the motive for any given act of animal cruelty, analogous to the human criminal/hero dichotomy, is imperative, the authors noted. For example, two boys may each kill a mouse. One boy lives on a farm and finds the mouse in a feed bin. The other boy lives in a city and the mouse that he kills is his sister's pet. The two boys live in demographically and culturally diverse sections of the country. The definition of *mouse* is determined in great part by that very diversity. As a result, and within the context of motive, there is a broad qualitative difference between the two acts of violence just cited. In fact, the difference is broad enough to suggest that only *one* act of cruelty may have been committed. In this context, the farm boy might be appropriately viewed as having eliminated a *pest* that could contaminate feed. The city boy, however, killed a *pet*, an animal that was cherished and loved by his sister and was thus, in Mead's words, a good animal.

Considering the implications of *motive* and *definition* as framed by Kellert and Felthous, however, it is conceivable that the farm boy may also have committed a cruel act. For example, did the farm boy kill the mouse swiftly and expediently, or did he torture the mouse and make it suffer? If the latter scenario was the case, not only would Kellert and Felthous have determined that the boy's act was indeed an act of cruelty, they would have interpreted the act as highly significant with respect to the correlation. Therefore, according to the criteria established by Kellert and Felthous, cruelty to animals can still be articulated as such even when cultural nuances can complicate the phenomenon.

The Present Study

The findings of many of the studies to date are inconclusive with respect to the relationship between cruelty to animals and human violence. There is widespread agreement among clinicians, researchers, and those who work in law enforcement, mental health, and social services that further investigation is needed. In the twenty-first century, violence in our society is very real, and it increasingly appears to be affecting children as well as adults (Heide, 1999). Furthermore, in many of the instances in which violent outbursts have made national news, prior acts of cruelty to animals were found to be part of the profile of the perpetrator of the violence.

The present study builds on the groundwork established by previous studies. Clearly, the research and orientation of Kellert and Felthous (1985) have served as conceptual and practical points of departure for numerous studies, including this one. These authors clearly defined the applicable variables and presented them within a perceptual framework that enhanced their meanings and implications. For example, the authors' precise definitions of motives for abuse considered within the cultural contexts within which they operate significantly broadened the conceptual parameters within which cruelty to animals might be understood as a *process* rather than as merely an *act*.

In the next chapter, evidence from previous studies that supports a relationship between cruelty to animals and human violence is critically reviewed. In the third and final chapter of part I, three theories that attempt to explain the link between animal cruelty in childhood and later violence toward people are presented. These two chapters provide the backdrop for the present study, which is the focus of part II.

A REVIEW OF THE RELATED LITERATURE

During the period between the 1960s and the present, a substantial amount of literature with respect to cruelty to animals and its relationship to human violence appeared. Some studies have focused specifically on the relationship of cruelty to animals to violence against humans, while others have included animal cruelty as one of several factors studied in the context of understanding violent behavior.

The conclusions of these studies have varied. Some have concluded that cruelty to animals is a significant factor, while others have found it to be insignificant. The latter studies have frequently cited such factors as familial violence and school and peer problems as more salient predictors of violent behavior. The literature, however, has often concluded that further research is needed to facilitate more meaningful understanding of this complex phenomenon. Verification has been a concern often raised in the literature.

Verification appears to have been a long-standing problem in the examination of the correlation between cruelty to animals and subsequent violence against people (see, e.g., Tapia, 1971; Wax & Haddox, 1974b; Felthous & Kellert, 1987). Verification problems have been the result of two fundamental difficulties. First, the lack of centralized information gathering among agencies, already cited, complicates any attempt to quantify and qualify the phenomenon. Second, self-reporting of acts of cruelty to animals and verification of past acts has remained problematic. Questions concerning cruelty to animals often have been omitted from critical processes such as the questioning of juvenile offenders, child abuse victims, and families in domestic-abuse shelter settings.

The literature focusing on animal cruelty and human violence has examined the correlation from various theoretical and applied perspectives. These perspectives have included such factors as motive, aggressive control, family dynamics, fascination with death, data verification, sexual and aggressive development processes, typologies such as that of the serial killer, violence prediction and intervention, psychotic versus sociopathic behavior, methodological refinement, and the precision of definition and measurement.

Although substantial, the literature focusing both on the triad and on the phenomenon of cruelty to animals as its own entity remains inconclusive. A more in-depth look at the research of Kellert and Felthous is in order because their methodological approach theoretically frames much of the research that has followed.

The Framers: Kellert and Felthous Revisited

Kellert and Felthous paid meticulous attention to the specific act of cruelty committed and to understanding the motive behind the act. They focused particularly on the dynamics of aggression and control and how these factors affect acts of cruelty against animals and the motives behind them. The authors also emphasized other factors and presented a multidimensional framework within which the phenomenon of cruelty to animals might be more rigorously examined. They addressed issues such as family dynamics, the frequency of acts committed by the offender, and the fascination between the boundary between life and death that was often cited as part of the dynamics of those who were cruel to animals.

Kellert and Felthous (1985) compared criminals and noncriminals with respect to cruelty to animals. Within the criminal group, the authors further distinguished between aggressive and nonaggressive criminals. They concluded that aggressive criminals committed cruelty to animals with greater frequency than nonaggressive criminals and noncriminals. Kellert and Felthous determined that frequency of acts of cruelty against animals became a decisive factor separating aggressive and nonaggressive criminals. Therefore, the authors determined that five or more acts of cruelty committed against animals was the decisive factor with respect to those more likely to become aggressive criminals. In this scenario, a cycle of violence escalated until it included human victims. The authors reported that Albert DeSalvo, the Boston Strangler, trapped dogs and cats, placed them in orange crates, and shot arrows through the boxes. One of DeSalvo's favorite childhood pastimes was to place a starving cat in an orange crate with a puppy and watch the cat attack the puppy and scratch its eyes out (Schechter & Everitt, 1996).

In addition to frequency, Kellert and Felthous addressed the importance of motive. Had they not examined motive, the overall result would be that any given act of cruelty would be equal to any other—an interpretation that would certainly have engendered far different conclusions. (For the nine motives cited by Kellert and Felthous, see chapter 1.)

The survey developed by Ascione, Thompson, and Black (1997), which was used as one of the two collection instrument tools in our study, applied the guidelines suggested by Kellert and Felthous. It addresses such factors as the type of animal abused (wild, farm, pet, or stray, and vertebrate or invertebrate) and provides quantification scales for such variables as frequency and severity of abuse. It serves as a vehicle for the practical application of the recommendations established by Kellert and Felthous. Seven of the nine motives of cruelty proposed by Kellert and Felthous (1985) are particularly important with respect to the correlation between animal cruelty and human cruelty as it is approached in this study. These seven motives have direct relevance to the profiling of three theories of offenders, the focus of discussion in chapter 3. They are:

1. to control an animal

2. to express aggression through an animal

3. to enhance one's own aggressiveness

4. to shock people for amusement

5. to retaliate against another person

6. displacement of hostility from a person to an animal

7. nonspecific sadism.

The remaining two motives (to retaliate against an animal, and to satisfy a prejudice against a species or breed) will be discussed separately, from the perspective of how they might offer insights into cruelty to animals that may or may not be relative to the correlation between animal cruelty and later cruelty to humans.

In their review of the literature, Felthous and Kellert (1987) constructed a conceptual continuum of the research to date and examined it with a critical eye. The authors summarized and evaluated the literature on cruelty to animals and its relationship to human violence. They noted the inconsistent findings represented by the research and suggested possible remedies to address these inconsistencies, such as improved verification techniques. Their review served as a critique to facilitate future research that might ultimately either validate or negate the proposed relationship.

The authors discussed nine studies that did not substantiate a relationship and four studies that did. They concluded that the relationship between cruelty to animals in childhood and later personal violence had not been demonstrated. They argued that this fact, in itself, however, neither discredited nor disproved a relationship. Instead, the authors suggested that problems with respect to the methodologies used in the studies accounted for a good deal of the resulting inconsistent findings. To emphasize this point, the authors asserted that most of the studies, particularly the ones that did not find an association, did not define the behavior of cruelty to animals. More importantly, they noted that a clearly articulated definition of personal aggression was seldom presented. In addition, some of the studies relied on interview reporting alone, without the use of clinical records; or, conversely, relied upon records without interviewing the subjects. Finally, the authors concluded that the discrepant findings that were derived from the interview process resulted from variation in the thoroughness of the interviews. In this vein, the authors asserted that "an interview schedule that taps several major life areas in which animals may be involved is more apt to elicit acts of cruelty in an individual's past than a schedule with just a few questions on animal cruelty" (Felthous & Kellert, 1987, p. 716). The authors concluded that replication studies applying the "minimum methodological rigor suggested here" (p. 716) were required.

Kellert and Felthous (1985) examined family dynamics and cited domestic violence as a contributing variable influencing cruelty to animals. The authors found that domestic violence in the families of aggressive criminals assumed many forms, although extreme paternal violence and alcoholism were especially common. Additionally, nonaggressive criminals and noncriminals who engaged in acts of animal cruelty often reported childhood physical abuse, frequent fights with fathers, and parental alcoholism.

Kellert and Felthous further noted that such offenders are often fascinated with the boundary between life and death. This finding is consistent with much of the literature addressing cruelty to animals as a component of cult activities, including those involving human sacrifice. In this regard, Raschke (1990) reported that confessed Missouri murderer Jim Hardy killed his high-school peer Steve Newberry as a sacrifice to Satan. Hardy asserted that killing Newberry was like killing any other animal. Hardy's apparent fascination with the kill included the aura of power and control that it represented, specifically the very power to choose and expedite death.

The specific factors of *aggression* and *control* cited by Kellert and Felthous (1985) have been cited in other studies as well. For example, Mead (1964) cited the conclusion drawn by homicide researchers Rosen, Satten, Mayman, and Menninger (1960) that extremely violent offenders exhibited a long-standing, sometimes lifelong, history of erratic control and aggressive impulses. These tendencies, combined with displacement, permitted these offenders to target both animals and humans. Mead further cited that Rosen et al. reported that these offenders brought to the murder scene a potential readiness to kill that was activated by the perception of the victim as representing a key figure in some past network of trauma, such as that resulting from child abuse.

Wax and Haddox: Sexual Polymorphy

The studies by Wax and Haddox (1974a; 1974b; 1974c) focused on the relationship of the triad in terms of subjects who had developed aggressive tendencies beginning in infancy. Wax and Haddox (1974c) reported that clinical observers have often described human behavior in terms of a set of interlocking need systems. These needs include "(1) nutrient intake, (2) oxygen intake, (3) water intake, (4) waste elimination, (5) temperature regulation, and (6) periods of sleep" (Wax & Haddox, 1974c, p. 102).

Wax and Haddox began their discussion by noting that infants must depend on others to meet their needs. A "gradient of tension" is associated with need gratification, and the tension is discharged when the infant's needs are met. In this model, homeostatic stability and pleasure are intertwined. The authors maintained that human sexuality operates in an analogous fashion to those fundamental needs in the interlocking need systems, because sexual arousal also involves a heightening of tension fol-lowed by a release of tension. According to Wax and Haddox, the stimuli required to facilitate tension release with respect to these various needs is highly individualized and is the result of developmental experiences in the life of each individual.

The authors related that, although sexual expression does not pre-dominate in the infant, it is present. For example, "male infants do achieve erections either spontaneously or from penile contact with objects" (p. 103). Therefore, infantile sexuality assumes many forms and is "polymor-phous" (p. 103). The authors concluded that polymorphous infantile sex-uality becomes especially important with respect to sexual perversion and related aberrant sexual behavior.

The study by Wax and Haddox added a *developmental* dimension to the examination of aggressive tendencies. On the basis of their findings, the authors described a polymorphous sex offender as representing a fu-sion of sexual and aggressive behavior. It was necessary for this type of of-fender to commit violence in order to achieve sexual release.

Wax and Haddox (1974c) described this developmental typology in their study conducted for the California Youth Authority. The authors served as clinical consultants and examined a total of forty-six cases that were referred to them during a six-month period. Each case study included substantial background documentation, including psychological and psy-chiatric testing and screening; essential medical, developmental, and judi-cial data; and parental and/or foster placement documentation. Six of the forty-six adolescents displayed all three elements of the triad. In these six cases, excessive cruelty to animals provided sexual release. Violence com-mitted against humans by these subjects had included rape and murder.

Four additional cases were considered to exhibit the triad but were not included in the study because complete documentation of one or more of the components was not possible. Although the authors believed that many youth authority subjects possessed the triad, denial of one or more of the symptoms by the subject was considered sufficient for exclusion, in accordance with the authors' previously expressed concern regarding the importance of verification (Wax & Haddox, 1974c).

The triad has been cited in several studies. Recent studies indicate that further research is required in light of the contradictory findings with re-spect to the predictive value of the triad. Lockwood and Church (1998) stressed the importance of continued study of the triad, particularly of its component of cruelty to animals, in terms of its preventative value thirty years after its proposal by MacDonald. The authors cited the words of Alan Brantley, a supervisory special agent with the Federal Bureau of Investigation (FBI), who concluded from his field experience that "animal cruelty is not a harmless venting of emotion in a healthy individual but rather it is a warning sign that this individual needs some sort of intervention" (p. 244).

The remaining seven sections of the literature review examine previous research on animal cruelty in terms of interpersonal violence in general and then, in its most extreme form, sexually oriented murderers and serial offenders. The review then discusses studies exploring animal cruelty as a predictor of future violence, recognizing that findings have often been confounded by weak methodological design. Research examining animal cruelty within the context of domestic violence, institutionalized violence, and human responsibility is presented. The review concludes with an extensive commentary on the literature, which sets the stage for understanding the present study.

Animal Cruelty and Interpersonal Violence

Arluke and Lockwood (1997) observed that during the last forty years, society's concerns have focused on the environment. The authors suggested that, in the next several years, society will focus on violence and that the dynamic of cruelty to animals represents an objectively definable behavior. The authors further suggested that cruelty to animals provides new perspectives with respect to the study of violence. They emphasized the need for standardization of reporting practices and tracking and greater articulation as to how victimology varies for different kinds of animals (e.g., by species as well as other factors such as owned versus stray, and wild versus tame versus domestic).

They noted that attention should be given to demographics, gender, and age with respect to perpetrators of cruelty to animals. The authors also proposed that noninstitutionalized populations must be examined with respect to the dynamic of cruelty to animals. They suggested that continued studies are necessary to better measure the relationship of frequency and severity of cruelty to animals as operational factors with respect to a progression of violence by perpetrators.

The following three studies did not focus on cruelty to animals. Rather, they addressed issues related to interpersonal violence that have direct implications for the study of the correlation between animal cruelty and violence against humans. The first, by Owens and Straus (1975), examined the concepts of culture and social behavior within the context of how humans treat each other. The authors analyzed data from a survey conducted in 1968 for the President's Commission on the Causes and Prevention of Violence. They used these data to investigate the relationship of three aspects of exposure to violence in childhood: observing violence, being a victim of violence, and committing violence. At the time of the survey, there was growing national concern about the high homicide rate in the United States. The U.S. rate was seven times higher than that of the second-ranking industrial nation, leading some observers to characterize the United States as having a "culture of violence" (Owens & Straus, 1975, p. 194).

Owens and Straus's study was concerned with interpersonal violence and did not examine the phenomenon of cruelty to animals. However, the authors concluded that violence "is a multifaceted phenomenon" and that "situations in which violent behavior occurs can be as widely varied as that of a parent spanking a child, two teenaged boys in a knife fight, a vigilante mob, or a massacre in a war" (p. 199). The authors expressed the need for precise definition of the variables they examined, as did Kellert and Felthous. Owens and Straus concluded that violence observed, received, or committed by a child resulted in the approval of the use of violence in adulthood, suggesting a continuum of violence.

The second study, by Justice, Justice, and Kraft (1974), examined such aggressive tendencies as fighting and found that *inadequate social skills* were significant indicators of violence. The authors conducted a systematic analysis of the literature between 1950 and 1971 and cited 188 references to predictors of interpersonal violence. These references were then analyzed for frequency of occurrence of symptoms or behavior patterns. In addition, the authors conducted 779 tape-recorded interviews with individuals in twenty-five professions who came into contact with troubled youth. Eight follow-up interviews were conducted. The authors concluded that fighting was the most commonly cited predictor of potential violence. The authors cited three additional predictors that were considered most significant: school problems, temper tantrums, and inability to get along with others. Although the authors concluded that social factors such as these were the most significant predictors of violence, they reported that cruelty to animals appeared fairly often in the follow-up case histories.

A third study, by Santtila and Haapasalo (1997), compared groups of homicidal, violent, and nonviolent offenders in Finland across a set of risk factors that included neurological disorders, early behavior problems, and abuse experiences. They found that a combination of risk factors differentiated homicide offenders from other offender groups. These factors included onset of alcohol abuse, prevalence of drug dependence, extent of physical abuse, and cruelty to animals. The authors emphasized that these factors in combination, rather than in isolation from one another, proved to be a better predictor of future violence.

Ascione (2001) provided a comprehensive overview of animal cruelty and its relationship to human violence on various levels, focusing on the psychiatric, psychological, and criminological research linking animal abuse to juvenile- and adult-perpetrated violence. Ascione characterized violent behavior as multidimensional and multidetermined. In his view, animal abuse as a possible precursor, or correlate of, interpersonal violence has received insufficient attention. Ascione referenced a study by Stone and Kelner (2000), for example, that explicitly excluded animal cruelty as a risk factor.

In his synthesis of the pertinent literature, Ascione discussed studies that found higher incidences of animal abuse in samples of children referred to mental health clinics (Achenbach, Howell, Quay, & Connors, 1991), violent youths (Youssef, Attia, & Kamel, 1999), and youths likely to be diagnosed as having conduct disorder (CD) (Loeber, Farrington, & Waschbusch, 1998) relative to their respective control groups. Loeber et al. suggested that cruelty to animals might be one of the first CD symptoms to appear in young children. Ascione concluded that "addressing cruelty to animals as a significant form of aggressive and antisocial behavior may add one more piece of the puzzle of understanding and preventing youth violence" (Ascione, 2001, p. 11).

Ascione also addressed animal abuse with respect to incarcerated subjects. A study by Schiff, Louw, and Ascione (1999) focused on a population of 117 men incarcerated in a South African prison. The authors found that 63.3 percent of the inmates incarcerated for aggressive crimes had committed prior acts of animal cruelty, whereas 10.5 percent of the inmates incarcerated for nonaggressive crimes had committed prior acts of animal cruelty (Ascione, 2001).

Ascione (2001) emphasized the importance of including information about animal abuse in assessments of youth at risk of committing interpersonal violence. Ascione noted, consistent with others before him (e.g., Reynolds & Kamphaus [1992]), that instruments used by teachers to assess children's problem behaviors seldom include animal abuse. Although teachers are unlikely to directly observe acts of animal cruelty committed by students, they may hear about such acts or read about them in written work. Accordingly, Ascione (2001) concurred with Dwyer, Osher, and Warger (1998) that these indirect observations should be taken seriously and serve as a signal for further assessment.

Although cruelty to animals is one of the fifteen symptoms of CD identified in the fourth edition of *Diagnostic and Statistical Manual of Mental Disorders* (DSM-IV), cruelty to animals does not appear in any of the categories under which juvenile offenders are classified, despite law enforcement's long-standing acknowledgment of the link between animal abuse and human violence (see, e.g., Schleuter, 1999). Ascione maintained that, although CD assessments are not typically designed to discover the reasons for a child's or adolescent's acts of cruelty toward animals, understanding the motivations for such behavior may be critical for designing effective intervention strategies (see, e.g., Agnew, 1998).

Ascione and Lockwood (2001) (as cited in Ascione, 2001) suggested that one model that could be used to develop an animal abuse assessment instrument is that used to assess firesetting. The authors reported that firesetting shares many features with animal abuse and that both are CD symptoms. Ascione noted that some children manifest both firesetting and cruelty to animals, as demonstrated in studies by Wooden and Berkey (1984) and Sakheim and Osborne (1994).

Ascione (2001) noted that the sexual abuse of animals has been given little attention in the research. Ascione pointed to an excellent theoretical overview of animal sexual abuse provided by Beirne (1997) and one of the few empirical studies available on this topic, by Wiegand, Schmidt, and Kleiber (1999). The paucity of literature is alarming given the likelihood that juvenile sex offenders, as noted by Lane in 1997, might sexually abuse animals in combination with other violent behavior toward them.

Four recent studies directly explored the relationship between animal cruelty and interpersonal violence. In the first of these studies, Miller (2001) emphasized the difficulties of quantifying the phenomenon of cruelty to animals in terms of its suspected relationship to interpersonal violence. The author cited problems with respect to definition, accountability, and a lack of research focus on the phenomenon. Miller provided an overview of the research and articles to date with respect to the relationship of cruelty to animals and conduct disorder in children in the United States. CD affects 2 to 9 percent of children in this country and has been found to be relatively stable through childhood and adolescence and into adulthood. Research has indicated that symptoms of CD (such as animal cruelty) might be a long-standing pattern of behavior that continues into adulthood and that earlier onset might indicate a poorer prognosis. Difficulties in diagnosis are compounded because cruelty to animals is under-reported and not every state considers animal cruelty to be a serious crime.

Miller reported that cruelty to animals is being increasingly viewed as a warning sign for potential violence. The author noted that, according to Lockwood and Church (1998), the FBI's Behavioral Sciences Unit teaches its members that "the investigation and prosecution of crimes against animals is an important tool for identifying people who are, or may become, perpetrators of violent crimes against people" (p. 241). Miller maintained that the available research (e.g., Felthous and Kellert, 1987) appears to support the position that abusive acts against socially valued animals (pets) are more likely associated with interpersonal violence than are abuses of less socially valued animals (e.g., rats). Furthermore, Miller asserted that the literature suggests an association between a pattern of cruelty to animals and a pattern of recurrent aggression against people.

Miller noted that researchers have attempted to ascertain the cause of animal cruelty and that some have cited a basic lack of empathy as a central factor. The author reported that in 1998, California became the first state in the country to require psychological counseling as a condition of probation for any person convicted of animal cruelty. However, Miller remarked that very little research has been conducted to identify effective interventions to reduce the frequency and severity of cruelty to animals. The author concluded that the phenomenon of cruelty to animals has received limited attention in the research literature to date, and that several areas of the phenomenon require further study. Miller concluded, first and foremost, that "a clear and consensual definition of animal cruelty is needed" (p. 745).

In a second study examining the link between animal cruelty and human violence, Luk, Staiger, Wong, and Mathai (1999) reported that persistent conduct problems that begin in childhood are a high-risk factor in the development of serious social and emotional adjustment problems in adolescence and adulthood, leading to impaired interpersonal relationships and social interactions. The authors queried whether cruelty to animals might be used as a marker of a subtype of persistent conduct problems predicting a poor outcome. They noted that several studies conducted in the 1960s and 1970s using a case report method found a link between cruelty to animals in childhood and adolescence and recurrent aggressive behavior in adulthood.

The authors conducted a reanalysis of previously collected data in order to investigate the significance of cruelty to animals. Two groups of children were initially selected. The first group was composed of 141 primary school children referred to a mental health service with symptoms suggestive of oppositional defiant/conduct disorder. The children were included in the sampling if they exhibited at least one symptom apart from cruelty to animals. Children who were "sometimes" or "definitely" cruel to animals made up the "clinical group" ($n = 40$); those who were not cruel to animals composed the "clinical control group" ($n = 101$). The second group of thirty-six children was recruited from the community as the "community control."

The interview and screening procedurals included the selected children, their parents, and, with parental permission, teachers. The children, between the ages of five and twelve, were assessed using a test battery of questionnaires for parents, teachers, and children on mental health symptoms, self-perception, demographics, and psychosocial factors. The two clinical samples were compared with the community sample. The cruelty to animals clinical sample had more conduct disorder symptoms than the noncruelty clinical sample. No significant differences were found between the two clinical subsamples with respect to gender, attention deficit hyperactivity disorder, internalization of symptoms, or psychosocial factors. The authors concluded that cruelty to animals appeared to be an indicator of a subgroup of conduct disorder that has a poor prognosis.

The authors noted that because their study was a reanalysis of existing data, they were unable to provide detailed data on the nature of cruelty to animals. They reported that cruelty to animals was reported in 28 percent of the cases of children with persistent conduct problems. The authors concluded that if this prevalence is confirmed by other studies, then cruelty to animals is underrecognized and a serious social issue. Moreover, they suggested that animal cruelty may serve as a marker of a subgroup of conduct disorder that has a poor prognosis.

Some studies supporting the correlation between animal cruelty and adult violence have suggested that cruelty to animals leads to a continuum of violence, ultimately directed against humans. The third study, by Arluke, Levin, Luke, and Ascione (1999), addressed this supposition. The authors reported that previous research had often assumed a "violence graduation hypothesis" whereby animal abusers were expected to escalate their way up from harming animals to harming people (Arluke et al., 1999, p. 963). The authors designed their study to test the graduation hypothesis. They cited social deviant theorists (e.g., Osgood, Johnston, O'Malley, & Bachman, 1988), who proposed that individuals who commit one form of deviance are likely to commit other forms as well, and in no particular time order. Contending that a self-reporting approach might encourage subjects to fabricate or exaggerate information, the authors chose an investigative approach whereby they reviewed official records in a sample of animal abusers who had come to the attention of the Massachusetts Society for the Prevention of Cruelty to Animals (MSPCA).

One hundred and fifty-three participants who had been prosecuted for at least one form of animal cruelty were selected; a search was conducted for case controls that would closely match the demographic backgrounds of the abusers. Using state computerized criminal records, both abusers and controls were tracked in the state's criminal justice records system. Results indicated that animal abusers were significantly more likely than control participants to be involved in some form of criminal behavior. The authors found that the animal abuse was no more likely to precede than to follow either violent or nonviolent offenses. Although the authors rejected the graduation hypothesis, they concluded that "as a flag of potential antisocial behavior—including but not limited to violence—isolated acts of cruelty toward animals must not be ignored by judges, psychiatrists, social workers, veterinarians, police, and others who encounter cases of abuse in their work" (Arluke et al., 1999, p. 968).

The authors cited limitations with respect to their study design. Use of official reports of single cases of abuse might have underrepresented episodes of animal abuse that may have preceded violent crimes committed by the subjects. The authors concluded that if they had instead studied repeated acts of abuse, it is possible that the graduation hypothesis might have been supported because "psychopathology may be more present in animal abusers who repeated offenses than in those who commit single acts of abuse" (Arluke et al., 1999, p. 968). This finding is in keeping with the position of Kellert and Felthous (1985) that frequency of acts of animal cruelty was an important factor with respect to support for the correlation.

A fourth study, by Gleyzer, Felthous, and Holzer (2002), tested the hypothesis that a history of substantial animal cruelty was associated with a diagnosis of antisocial personality disorder (APD), a diagnosis that has long been associated with repeat violent offenders. Study participants included forty-eight men with a history of animal cruelty during childhood and forty-eight men with no such history. The authors found that cruelty to animals was significantly associated with APD, antisocial personality traits, and polysubstance abuse but not with mental retardation, psychotic disorders, and alcohol abuse. The authors concluded that long-term prospective studies of behaviorally disordered and aggressive children and youths should include animal cruelty not merely as a behavioral sign of APD but also as a probe for specific psychopathologic dimensions of psychopathy. The authors also recommended that clinicians examine the frequency, severity, and nature of cruelty, the types of animals victimized, and the motivations behind the mistreatment.

Some of the more recent literature has focused on the interrelationship of human and nonhuman lives. In this view, humans and animals are viewed in terms of their connections to one another within an ecological framework. Ascione (1999) explored this paradigm.

Ascione introduced his article by citing the murderous rampage on October 1, 1997, at Pearl High School, Pearl, Mississippi, perpetrated by Luke Woodham, who murdered his mother and two high school students and injured seven other students. Ascione reported that Woodham had allegedly written in his diary about the torture and killing of his own dog, Sparkle. The animal was reportedly beaten with clubs, doused with lighter fluid, set on fire, and thrown into a pond. Ascione reported that Woodham's diary entries included the words, "I'll never forget the sound of her breaking under my might. . . . I will never forget the howl she made. . . . It sounded almost human. We laughed and hit her more" (Ascione, 1999, p. 50).

The author noted that animal abuse does not inevitably lead to interpersonal violence and that there is "a relation and not necessarily a causal one" between the two (p. 51). Ascione cautioned, however, that we must come to a better understanding of the circumstances in which animal cruelty is related to interpersonal violence for the sake of both animals and people. Ascione suggested that ecological theory (as explained in Bronfenbrenner & Morris, 1997) might be enlisted as a conceptual model because it includes "the societal and cultural elements of beliefs and practices in which human development is embedded" (Ascione, 1999, p. 51). Animals might be relevant in an ecological framework. For example, Ascione theorized that companion animals might be viewed as "symbiotic members of human families, stray animals as participants in neighborhood and community ecosystems, and societal views about the treatment of farm animals and wildlife as part of our cultural environment" (p. 52).

The author further suggested that when the interrelations of law enforcement, mental health workers, educators, and clergy are acknowledged and strengthened, both animals and humans benefit. Ascione noted that increased attention has been focused on the "overlaps between child abuse and neglect, domestic violence, community violence, and animal abuse" (p. 50) during the past decade. He concluded that "the links between animal abuse and interpersonal violence are ripe for research at all ecological levels, from the individual to society and culture" (pp. 57–58).

Animal Cruelty and Sexually Oriented Murderers and Serial Offenders

In this section, we look at studies that examine the correlation between animal cruelty and human violence in its most extreme form. The most provocative research on the relationship between animal cruelty and violence against people has come from the results of studies that have focused on extremely violent offenders, including serial offenders. One such study, by Ressler, Burgess, Hartman, Douglas, and McCormack (1998), supported the significance of cruelty to animals as a predictor of future violence against humans. The authors focused on sexual crime. The study was prompted by a growing concern within law enforcement about "motiveless" homicides. Crimes committed without apparent motive were especially difficult to solve. The FBI responded by devising a typology whereby the crime scene was examined in an effort to establish patterns and ultimately lead to a "profile" of the offender. In this venue, a psychological understanding of the offender was critical and introduced a new element to law enforcement investigative procedures.

Ressler and his colleagues conducted an analysis based on information about the crime scenes of thirty-six sexually oriented murders by using information from interviews and official records. The purpose of the study was to compare behavioral and symptomatic differences between subjects who had been sexually abused and those subjects who had not been sexually abused. The study differentiated the specific developmental stage(s) when abuse had occurred: childhood and/or adolescence. The authors looked for evidence of the triad. Of the three components of the triad, only cruelty to animals and firesetting were found to be statistically significant. Those subjects who were sexually abused in adolescence were more likely than unabused subjects to report firesetting. The authors found no significance with respect to firesetting among those subjects who had been sexually abused during childhood. However, the authors found that during childhood and adolescence, a significantly greater proportion of the subjects who had been sexually abused had committed cruelty to animals than subjects who had not been sexually abused. There was no statistically significant difference between the two groups with respect to cruelty to animals committed during adulthood. A significantly greater proportion of the subjects who had been sexually abused, however, had committed cruelty to children. This study suggests that among offenders who had been sexually abused, the cruelty that they committed may be part of a continuum that started with animals, escalated to children, and culminated in sexual homicide.

The study by Ressler et al. dramatically influenced the methodologies established by the FBI's Behavioral Sciences Unit. The correlation between animal cruelty and violence toward humans was viewed as an applicable tool for use by law enforcement. The study also used precise definitions and complied with the stringent methodology advocated by Kellert and Felthous (1985).

Perhaps the greatest significance of this study is that it appeared to lend support to the position held by Hellman and Blackman that cruelty to animals had, in fact, useful *predictive* potential. Coupled with Margaret Mead's prophetic warning that "one of the most dangerous things that can happen to a child is to kill or torture an animal and get away with it" (Lockwood & Hodge, 1998, p. 80), the phenomenon of cruelty to animals has been imbued with global significance. Mead, an anthropologist who had studied diverse cultures, determined that cruelty to animals was significant cross-culturally. Mead (1964) reemphasized the point when she asserted that, with respect to cruelty to animals committed by a child, "A failure of punishment here, when there is a cultural reliance on teaching and learning, can be as fatal or possibly even more fatal, than too violent punishment" (p. 21).

Studies such as the one by Ressler et al. indicated that cruelty to animals might be not only a predictor of violence against humans, but also a predictor of violence against humans in its most extreme forms. Cruelty to animals as part of the profile of the serial killer has appeared in the literature frequently. Norris (1988) included extraordinary cruelty to animals in his list of twenty-one patterns of episodic aggressive behavior (p. 223). Douglas and Olshaker (1995) also noted past acts of cruelty to animals in many of their profiles of serial offenders, including that of David Berkowitz. They concluded that the serial killer "has most probably experimented with torturing small animals and may do it regularly" (p. 350). Holmes and Holmes (1996) reported that cruelty to animals often appeared in the backgrounds of "mysopeds" (sadistic pedophiles).

Certainly, some researchers appear to have followed the advice of Kellert and Felthous (1985) by using the improved methodologies they recommended with respect to the investigation into the relationship of cruelty to animals and later human violence. Similarly, some of the more recent research on serial killers and child abuse demonstrates an analogous attention to definition and methodological precision. This is a highly positive development given the fact that child abuse has been cited as a developmental precursor to antisocial impulses and that these same impulses have been suggested to be precursors to both animal abuse and violence directed against humans. Keeney and Heide (1995) refined the definition of serial murder to the following: "Serial murder is the premeditated murder of three or more victims committed over time, in separate incidents, in a civilian context, with the murder activity being chosen by the offender" (p. 304). They also reported that "Serial murderers wear many guises. They can be the quiet, single, next-door neighbor; the pudgy teenaged babysitter in a small town; the night-shift nurse in a big-city hospital" (p. 1). With respect to child maltreatment, Heide (1992) precisely defined the components of child abuse and neglect.

Support for the significance of the triad with respect to violent criminality is found in the previously cited study by Ressler et al. and in the literature with respect to serial killers, such as the work by Norris (1988). Hickey (2002) also provided support for the correlation. The author, an expert on serial murderers and their victims, noted that some serial killers have displayed delight in harming animals. He maintained, however, that more appear to have enjoyed vivisection and the exploration of dead animals. Hickey noted, "In America, a pet can be the object of affection or the target of displaced scorn" (Hickey, 2002, p. 100). He cited the nine motivations for the childhood maltreatment of animals identified by Felthous and Kellert (1987), as well as Mead's (1964) often quoted warning, "One of the most dangerous things that can happen to a child is to kill or torture and animal and not he held responsible" (p. 101). After noting that animal abuse has been included in the *Diagnostic and Statistical Manual of Mental Disorders'* diagnoses of conduct disorder since 1987, Hickey concluded that "without proper intervention, children may graduate to more serious abuses including violence against people" (p. 101).

Wright and Hensley (2003) examined the possible link between childhood animal cruelty and serial murder by using social learning theory, specifically examining the graduation hypothesis. The authors noted that since the late 1970s, the FBI and other law enforcement officials have considered animal cruelty to be a possible indicator of future serial murder. The authors observed that very little academic attention had focused on the childhood characteristics of serial killers. Rather, most of the literature to date focused on definitions and adult motivations of serial murder.

Wright and Hensley used five cases of serial killers to illustrate the relationship between animal cruelty engaged in during childhood and subsequent violence against people. The authors selected these cases because of the extensive information available on these serial killers. They cautioned against concluding that these five represent "an exhaustive list of serial killers who have committed childhood animal cruelty" (p. 76). They noted that, of the 354 cases of serial killers that they had examined, seventy-five (21 percent) were known to have engaged in acts of cruelty to animals during childhood.

The authors suggested that killing animals may have enabled these individuals to "graduate" to killing humans. The authors reflected, "Each serial murderer in this study seemed to transfer the frustration they received from their mothers or other adults toward weaker animals. The abusive behavior continued until the men eventually turned their attention to humans" (p. 85). The authors said, "If killing animals made them feel good, the next logical step for further gratification was humans" (p. 85). The authors further noted that these five serial killers used the same methods on their human victims that they had used to kill animals. Wright and Hensley concluded by saying that more research on the graduation hypothesis is needed.

Animal Cruelty as a Predictor of Future Criminality: Verification as a Confounding Factor

Studies that have examined the phenomenon of cruelty to animals by comparing violent and nonviolent populations remain of special interest because some, such as that by Hellman and Blackman (1966), supported the predictive value of the triad. A finding that cruelty to animals is significantly linked to future violence against humans would have broad implications not only for the criminal justice system but also for the many institutions and agencies that serve both children and animals.

Studies that compare violent and nonviolent groups must incorporate rigorous standards that clearly define the two groups. For example, definitions of *violent* and *nonviolent* must be clearly operationalized and verified. Findings from studies that used vague definitions for critical variables have questionable utility. This section reviews several studies in which findings were inconclusive owing to methodological imprecision. These design study flaws included (1) the failure to verify self-reported information, particularly as it relates to violent and criminal behavior; (2) exclusive reliance on material in case files as indicating the existence or nonexistence of childhood behavior such as enuresis, firesetting, and cruelty to animals; (3) reliance on subjects' assessments of childhood physical abuse and failure to ask about specific objective indicators that measure specific physically abusive behaviors; (4) precise definitions of acts of animal cruelty; and (5) subjects' perceptions of acts of cruelty.

A study by Climent, Hyg, and Erwin (1972) examined cruelty to animals within the context of criminal versus violent behavior. This study included a sampling of emergency room patients who were brought or came on their own to Boston City Hospital. Two groups were extracted from this population, a violent group (the study group) and a nonviolent group (the control group). A violent patient was defined as one with a chief complaint of violent behavior and with a reported history of severe violent acts. A nonviolent patient was defined as an individual who was at the emergency room to be treated for an orthopedic ailment and who reported no history of actions of adult violence. No confirmation by a witness was required, and the two groups were distinguished by self-reporting only.

The authors concluded that criminal and violent behavior should be examined as *separate* behaviors and that criminal behavior was related to *cultural* factors whereas violent behavior was related to *individual* factors. No differences were found between the two groups with regard to sleepwalking, sleep talking, nail biting, thumb sucking, difficulty in talking, childhood stealing, hyperactivity, frequent nightmares, pyromania, enuresis, or cruelty to animals. The results, therefore, indicated that cruelty to animals, whether operative on its own or as a component of the triad, was insignificant in terms of its relationship to human violence. The authors expressed concern about verification in light of the limitations of a sample selected in the manner described. As a result, they suggested that the triad, as described by Hellman and Blackman, required further study.

Two studies examined the predictive value of animal cruelty and criminality. In the first study, Shanok et al. (1983) focused on a comparison of the case histories of delinquent and nondelinquent adolescent psychiatric inpatients. The authors determined that the three behaviors noted in the literature as associated with delinquency (the triad) did not distinguish the delinquents from the nondelinquents. The study focused on twenty-nine delinquent and twenty-five nondelinquent adolescent males. The authors concluded that 20.7 percent of the delinquents had been enuretic beyond age four, as had 25 percent of the nondelinquents. Firesetting characterized 24.1 percent of the delinquents and 18.2 percent of the nondelinquents. Cruelty to animals was not mentioned in any of the delinquent histories and was mentioned in only 8.3 percent of the nondelinquent histories. Obviously, the triad was found to be an insignificant factor. It must be suggested, however, that problems with respect to verification might have been operative in this study, given the investigators' sole reliance on materials in subjects' case files. The potentially covert nature of acts of cruelty to animals, as compared to firesetting and enuresis, combined with the historical tendency to disregard cruelty to animals committed by children, particularly by disturbed children, as "things kids do" might well have inhibited appropriate documentation. Therefore, the findings should be viewed with caution.

In the second study, Miller and Knutson (1997) compared two groups of subjects, one composed of 314 inmates incarcerated for felonies in a prisoner classification center within the Iowa Department of Corrections system, and the second composed of 308 university students at the University of Iowa, in order to assess and compare the relationship between abusive childhood environments and exposure to animal cruelty. Both groups were administered self-report questionnaires. The authors noted that exposure to, and/or perpetration of, childhood cruelty to animals had been associated with the emergence of antisocial behavior, citing, among others, Kellert and Felthous (1985).

The authors reported that the study's analyses of the measurement of childhood physical abuse were confounded by many of the incarcerated subjects' failure to identify reported abuse as abuse. For example, slightly fewer than 60 percent of the respondents who met a conservative criterion for having been abused actually labeled themselves as abused. Furthermore, consistent with a pattern of apparent reluctance to label disciplinary experiences as abusive, the authors reported that six of the twenty-one subjects who required medical services because of parental acts failed to label themselves as having been physically abused.

The authors reported that the results of the study were consistent with the hypothesis that severely punitive childhood backgrounds can play a role in the ontogeny of antisocial behavior in general, and aggressive and violent behavior in particular. However, the authors also reported that the subject group charged with homicide more closely approximated the disciplinary background of the nonviolent groups. The authors suggested that this phenomenon may be explained by the fact that most homicides are "crimes of passion" (Miller & Knutson, 1997, p. 73). The authors reported that 66 percent of the incarcerated respondents reported some exposure to animal cruelty. The composite animal cruelty score consisted of the sum of responses to specific acts of cruelty—for example, being forced to hurt an animal or killing a stray or pet animal.

In the sample of university students, the authors found that 10.1 to 18.8 percent (depending on the scales used) of the students met the criteria set for physical abuse. Like the incarcerated group, the university students often failed to identify abuse as abuse. The authors found that reports of childhood exposure to acts of lethal or nonlethal animal cruelty were not uncommon. They reported that, although 48.4 percent of the university subjects reported some exposure to animal cruelty, approximately 57 percent of those reporting such exposure reported only witnessing such acts. Ten subjects reported killing their pets (not euthanasia) and forty-four (14.3 percent) of the subjects reported killing stray animals. The authors noted, however, that seven subjects (2.3 percent) reported that they had been charged with a felony and fifty-one (16.6 percent) reported being charged with a misdemeanor. When the subjects reporting misdemeanors and felonies were combined, there was a significant association between the reports of childhood histories of exposure to animal cruelty and being charged with a crime.

The authors concluded that the results of the two experiments support the hypothesis that punitive childhood backgrounds are common in persons convicted of felonious acts in general and violent behavior in particular. The authors indicated that the study results did not permit a determination as to whether animal cruelty is importantly related to either antisocial behavior or childhood maltreatment. The authors qualified their findings by maintaining that the definition of cruelty to animals had not been clearly developed in the literature to date. In addition, they noted that the study had only asked subjects to report specific acts and experiences with respect to animal cruelty and had not asked them to characterize the acts in any way. Therefore, the study did not reveal any information as to whether respondents viewed their own behavior or the behavior of others as cruel to animals or as normative. In this regard, verification of cruelty to animals as "cruelty" could not be determined. As a result, a viable test of the correlation was not possible.

Animal Cruelty and Domestic Violence

In this section, we look at studies that examine animal cruelty and violence against humans in the context of domestic violence. Findings from these studies have been mixed.

Kellert and Felthous (1985) examined the significance of family dynamics with respect to the development of aggressive tendencies. The authors cited domestic violence as a confusing variable with respect to cruelty to animals. Five earlier studies focused on home *environmental factors* as the key causes of violence committed by children. The findings of these studies either did not investigate, or did not find support for, the relationship of cruelty to animals (either as a single phenomenon or as part of the triad) as a precursor to human violence.

The first study, by Bender (1959), portrayed the homicidal adolescent as an unwanted child with an underdeveloped ego resulting from oral and maternal deprivation. The author included in her study objective clinical criteria such as IQ scores and EEG abnormalities along with environmental factors. A second study, by Easson and Steinhilber (1961), reinforced Bender's portrait of the homicidal adolescent as the product of parental deprivation and dysfunction. The homicidal adolescent was presented as coming from a family with a weak and distant father and an aggressive and destructive mother.

A third study, by Tapia (1971), reported that the most common factor shared by eighteen subjects who had committed acts of cruelty to animals was a chaotic home with aggressive parental models. Tapia concluded that these subjects as a group showed many other aggressive tendencies, such as destructiveness, bullying, fighting, stealing, and firesetting.

A fourth study, by Sendi and Blomgren (1975), looked at three groups of adolescent males. The first group was composed of ten adolescents who had been accused of murder. The second group consisted of ten adolescents who had unsuccessfully attempted homicide or threatened murder. The third group, considered a control group by the authors, consisted of ten adolescents randomly selected from hospitalized patients suffering from such psychiatric problems as schizophrenia. The authors specifically investigated such factors as an unfavorable home; parental brutality, particularly that imposed by the father; exposure to violence or murder; seduction by a parent; and sexual inhibition. The authors reported that the triad, which was equally distributed among the three groups, was not present in a global form in any patient and that each patient had, in general, only one or two of the signs. The authors concluded that environmental factors were most important in terms of both predisposition to violence and reinforcement of violent behavior, including homicidal behavior.

Similar to the study by Sendi and Blomgren (1975), a fifth study, by Lewis, Shanok, Grant, and Ritvo (1983), found that domestic violence, specifically that imposed upon the family by a violent father, was the most important factor in predicting violence. The authors studied two groups of children including both males and females. One group was composed of homicidally aggressive subjects and the other of nonhomicidal subjects. The authors concluded that the triad was insignificant as a predictive factor. They found that the 14 percent of homicidally aggressive subjects had a history of cruelty to animals compared to 3 percent among the nonhomicidal group.

The five articles discussed above found no relationship between animal cruelty and human violence among children and adolescents in chaotic homes. Numerous studies conducted from the 1980s to the present time have found cruelty to animals to be a compelling factor operative in the complex dynamics of familial dysfunction and abuse. The following four studies are examples of those that found cruelty to animals to be an important variable with respect to domestic violence.

The first study, by DeViney, Dickert, and Lockwood (1983), was conducted to establish behavior patterns toward animals in abusive families and to examine the care of pets within these families. The treatment of animals was surveyed in fifty-three families in which child abuse had occurred. Patterns of pet ownership, attitudes toward pets, and quality of veterinary care did not differ greatly from comparable data from the general public. Abuse of pets by a family member, however, had taken place in 60 percent of the child-abusing families.

This study clearly defined criteria of cruel acts. These range from observable or reported pain or suffering due to forms of discipline beyond those commonly accepted in American society to failure to provide basic care, such as adequate shelter and nutrition. In this regard, the authors clearly distinguished between abuse and neglect, the same terms applicable to the treatment of children. The authors determined that there were several parallels between the treatment of children and the treatment of pets within child-abusing families, suggesting that animal abuse may be an indicator of other family problems. In this vein, the authors concluded that in their sample of pet-owning child abusers, 88 percent of the families in which physical abuse took place also had animals that were abused. According to the authors, their findings suggested that it might be helpful to review the role of pets in these families as part of the therapeutic process.

A second study, by Ascione (1998a), also examined cruelty to animals within the context of domestic violence. The author suggested that, considering the growing concern in the United States about neighborhood or community violence and its impact on children, the dynamic of family violence should be afforded greater attention because violence within the family is the least escapable type of violence for a child. Ascione noted that many studies (e.g., Arkow, 1996; DeViney et al., 1983) had explicitly included the torture or destruction of a pet with respect to emotional abuse suffered by the child. Ascione interviewed thirty-eight women at a shelter for battered partners in Utah. Of these, 74 percent reported current pet ownership and 71 percent of these reported that their male partner had threatened to kill and/or had actually killed one or more of the pets. Of the women with pets, 18 percent reported that concern for their animals' welfare had prevented them from coming to the shelter earlier. The author concluded that, although his study did not include a comparison sample of nonbattered or battered women who were not currently in shelters, the substantial rate of partner cruelty to animals was a matter of serious concern. Ascione noted that, in general, only occasionally did specific questions related to animal abuse appear in domestic violence questionnaires or checklists.

A third study, by Quinlisk (1999), began with the author's reflections on her first day on the job as a freshly graduated counselor at a local battered women's shelter. The author recalled advising a young woman that it was best that she go back home. The woman then presented a photo showing her husband cutting off her beloved dog's ears with a pair of garden shears (p. 168). The author noted, "Twelve years and thousands of stories later, I am no longer as shockable" (p. 168). Quinlisk reported that after attending a conference, "Tangled Web: The Connection between Domestic Violence, Child Abuse and Animal Cruelty," sponsored by the La Crosse Community Coalition against Violence (CCAV) and presented by the Humane Society of the United States, she and colleagues created a survey to investigate the relationship between animal abuse and domestic violence. The findings of the survey indicated that in 67 percent of cases, women seeking shelter from domestic violence had witnessed animal abuse perpetrated by an abusive partner and that children had been present 43 percent of the time. Furthermore, the survey indicated that in 57 percent of the cases in which the children witnessed abuse, the mothers reported that the children themselves ultimately became abusers of animals.

The author reported that "although it is now widely accepted that children witnessing domestic violence frequently grow up to become either perpetrators or victims of violence according to their gender, these findings would seem to indicate a further continuance of animal cruelty as well" (Quinlisk, 1999, p. 170). The author also reported, however, that several women indicated that their children became protective and caring animal lovers because of the abuse they had witnessed. This finding raised the issue of *empathy*, a variable that proved to be highly significant with respect to the study investigated in this book. Quinlisk concluded that research needs to determine how to facilitate empathetic responses rather than violent imitation. She recommended that domestic violence shelters screen carefully with respect to client concerns regarding any animals in the household and that they network with area veterinarians, animal shelters, and boarding facilities so that safe housing might be provided for animals of families fleeing violence.

In a fourth study, Flynn (1999) investigated the link between animal abuse in childhood and the maintaining of favorable attitudes in young adulthood with respect to violence against children and women in families. The author noted that the physical punishment of children enjoys strong normative support in this country and that three out of four Americans approve of spanking. Flynn noted that, in contrast, Americans strongly oppose hitting their wives, and, as of 1994, only 10 percent of Americans could envision circumstances in which a husband would be justified in slapping his wife.

In Flynn's study, a questionnaire was completed by 267 undergraduate students enrolled in a southeastern university in 1997. Animal abuse was defined as (1) killing a pet, (2) killing a stray or wild animal, (3) hurting or torturing an animal to tease it or cause it pain, (4) touching an animal sexually, and (5) having sex with an animal. Behaviors such as killing an animal for food (farm animals intended for slaughter), hunting, and mercy killing were not counted as abuse because they are considered by many to be socially approved behaviors. The study found that 17.6 percent of the respondents reported at least one act of animal abuse, most commonly killing a stray animal. Respondents who had abused an animal during childhood or adolescence had significantly more favorable attitudes toward corporal punishment, even after controlling for the effects of childhood spanking, race, biblical literalism, and gender. Those with histories of animal cruelty were also more likely to approve of a husband slapping his wife (three to one) than respondents who had never committed abuse.

Duncan and Miller (2002) conducted the most comprehensive literature survey to date of studies that examine the effect of an abusive family context on childhood animal cruelty and adult violence. They examined available studies on this topic, including "child clinical samples, juvenile offenders, adult violent offenders, and adult aggressive psychiatric samples" (p. 367). Their review indicated that "Some of the specific abusive and adverse family contextual factors found to be associated with childhood animal cruelty and adult violence include child abuse, paternal alcoholism, paternal availability, domestic violence, and parental animal cruelty" (p. 371). They also presented research that suggested "an association between a dysfunctional and negative home environment, childhood animal cruelty, and adult violence" (p. 371). Duncan and Miller concluded that their review clearly underscored the need to understand the influence of an abusive family context on childhood animal cruelty and adult violence.

Two significant developments in measurement hold great promise in investigating the link between animal cruelty and domestic violence. Lewchanin and Zimmerman (2000) developed a manual to assist mental health clinicians involved in the evaluation of children and adolescents referred because of animal cruelty. The manual follows Ascione's definition of animal cruelty, which states that animal cruelty is a "socially unacceptable behavior that intentionally causes unnecessary pain, suffering, or distress to and/or death of an animal" (Lewchanin & Zimmerman, 2000, p. 6).

The authors remarked that even before the tragedy of Columbine High, President Bill Clinton had ordered Attorney General Janet Reno to form a task force to investigate the possible links between violence to animals and violence to people. The authors cautioned that, while childhood cruelty to animals does not inevitably lead to later violence against people, there does appear to be an association between animal cruelty and other antisocial behaviors, which could include violence. The authors further noted that since 1987, the *Diagnostic and Statistical Manual* of the American Psychiatric Association has considered animal cruelty as an important indicator of a child's mental health status.

Guymer, Mellor, Luk, and Pearse (2001) recently developed a screening instrument called the Children's Attitudes and Behaviors toward Animals (CABTA). This instrument, which was field-tested in three phases, distinguishes between types of animal cruelty. The CABTA examines *typical* and *malicious* cruelty to animals and is a reliable and valid tool for identifying cruelty to animals. Malicious cruelty to animals is a poor prognostic indicator among conduct-disordered children.

The discussion so far has focused on acts of cruelty committed by individuals. In the next section, attention focuses on institutionalized forms of animal cruelty.

Institutionalized Cruelty to Animals

Grandin (1988) defined and analyzed the treatment of animals by the employees of slaughter plants and auction markets. The author reported that out of twenty-five slaughter plants visited, fourteen rated good to excellent with respect to employee behavior toward animals. Acts of deliberate cruelty committed on a regular basis occurred at eight of the plants, and routinely rough handling occurred at three of the plants. Grandin reported that 21 percent of the auction markets exhibited excellent handling of animals, whereas 32 percent exhibited rough or cruel handling of animals.

Grandin's study is of special interest because it focuses on cruelty to animals within the context of a culturally and institutionally sanctioned form of animal *use* (farm animals slaughtered for human consumption). Obviously, the use of farm animals for this purpose is species specific, and not, in itself, considered to be cruel. However, the similar use of other species of animals, particularly companion animals (namely, dogs and cats) would be considered acts of animal cruelty in American culture. Therefore, Grandin's study underscores the importance of cultural practices and precepts that affect the treatment of animals by humans. The significance of Grandin's study is that it articulates cruelty to animals as a phenomenon apart from their eventual slaughter and establishes a conceptual framework within which the humane treatment of these types of animals might be furthered. This study implied that humans have a responsibility to treat animals humanely, even when the primary purpose of the animals in question is to provide a product for human use.

Grandin's study alluded to the fact that human perception of animals is a key cultural factor with respect to the manner in which humans conceptualize and use animals. The concept of *doubling*, as defined by Lifton (1986), provides significant insight into these conceptual processes. In his book *The Nazi Doctors,* Lifton addressed the perceptual contradictions operative in the minds of the Auschwitz doctors who selected those to be killed and conducted the killing. He examined the doctors' dichotomous thinking that permitted them to simultaneously be loving husbands and fathers and efficient killers. Lifton defined this type of thinking as "doubling" and said that it permitted the doctors "to select for the gas chamber without seeing themselves as killers" (p. 151). Lifton asserted that for the doctors, "killing became the prerequisite for healing" (p. 150). In this view, the doctors perceived themselves as "curing the Nordic race by ridding it of its dangerous Jewish infection" (p. 150). According to Lifton, it was this conceptual reversal that permitted the Nazi doctors to perceive themselves as *healers* even as they killed, much like modern physicians who seek to kill the cancer that invades and devastates the bodies of their patients. Likewise, the Nazi doctors attempted to cure the Nordic race of the Jewish "carriers of death" (p. 151).

Obviously, sensitivity and caution must be applied when parallels are drawn between the treatment of animals and that of humans. A case in point is the controversy that was ignited by Spiegel's 1988 book, *The Dreaded Comparison.* The book focused on what Spiegel perceived as the analogous treatment suffered by slaves and animals and compared racism with speciesism. Although Spiegel's book was applauded by some distinguished African Americans, such as Alice Walker, the book enraged others. Walker defended Spiegel's comparison by emphasizing the universality of pain. In Walker's preface to the book, she asserted that "animals were not made for humans any more than black people were made for whites or women for men" (p. 14). Although more than a decade has passed since the publication of *The Dreaded Comparison,* the type of controversy that Spiegel engendered continues with respect to both the use and the abuse of animals.

Returning to the study by Grandin (1988) and Lifton's (1986) concept of doubling, it would seem that doubling is indeed a critical process at work in the minds of humans with respect to their treatment of animals. Indeed, doubling provides the conceptual parameters for humans not only to define but also to *re-create* animals for their own uses. In this view, pigs become *ham,* calves become *veal,* cows become *beef,* squirrels become *pests,* and deer become *trophies.* It might be argued that in these cases the process of doubling is not carried through to conceptual completion, and thus conceptual reversal. The animals mentioned are either farm or wild animals, and thus they are not animals that have typically become endeared to humans as pets.

Such doubling might be best illustrated by considering for a moment the treatment of dogs and cats in American society. Millions of pets share the homes and even the beds of their human companions. They are loved and nurtured. They are provided veterinary care and even day care. When they die, they are mourned by their human companions as if they were family members. Certainly, many dogs and cats are treated like adored children. Yet, millions of homeless dogs and cats, puppies and kittens, are killed each year in animal control facilities because they are unwanted, a public nuisance, unadoptable, or excess animals. Ironically, the same individuals who conduct the killing by day often go home to their beloved pet dogs and cats at night—an appropriate example of doubling taken to conceptual completion, and thus conceptual reversal. Clearly, the power of the human mind to compartmentalize is a critical tool operative in the treatment of both animals and humans by humans. This discussion underscores the critical responsibility of society, veterinarians, and existing institutions that deal with animals to prevent animal cruelty.

Animal Cruelty and Human Responsibility

The issue of responsibility was raised by Arkow (1998). Arkow investigated cruelty to animals within the context of whether or not veterinarians had a legal and/or ethical responsibility to report suspected abuse, given "compelling evidence confirming intuitions that cruelty to animals, when perpetrated by children, might be a predictor of future antisocial behavior" (p. 409). Arkow suggested that because veterinarians are trained to be animal care professionals and not human mental health providers, the privilege of privacy normally afforded by the patient–doctor relationship might not apply to them. He believed that veterinarians, if they are inclined to get involved at all, might do so by contacting an animal shelter or animal control facility rather than the police or mental health service providers. Accordingly, Arkow researched the legal parameters of humane and animal control officers to determine their legal responsibility.

The author found that there were not only varying legal opinions as to their appropriate roles and authority, but that there was also conceptual confusion. For example, Arkow reported that no state officials considered humane agents or animal control officers "police or peace officers" (Arkow, 1998, p. 411). In many parts of the country, however, these "officers" perform analogous functions such as conducting investigations, assisting in filing formal charges, taking into custody abused or neglected animals, and so on. With respect to veterinarians, Arkow reported a similar conceptual and legal dichotomy on the part of the legal community. In fifteen states, veterinarians were not considered to be "health practitioners," "medical professionals," or practitioners of the "healing arts" (p. 411). In this view, veterinarians were not included in child abuse reporting because the child would not have been observed in the veterinarian's "professional capacity or within the scope of his or her employment" (p. 411).

Arkow concluded that including veterinarians in the reporting process would benefit all concerned: the animals that were subject to abuse, the abusing families that required intervention, and the veterinarians, who, as a result of their inclusion in the process, might be "perceived to be more in parity with physicians, dentists, and others in health care" (p. 412). Arkow also emphasized the potentially important role of humane officers and shelters in helping abused children. He concluded that child abuse victims might "find solace and healing in the veterinary or shelter environment" (p. 412). Therefore, the author concluded that both veterinarians and humane officers were vital links in the prevention of, and intervention in, abuse of both children and animals.

Arkow's study focused not only on animal and child abuse per se but also on how these types of abuse affect the development of antisocial impulses and behavior. He cited numerous cases of serial killers who had abused animals, including Albert DeSalvo, who in his youth shot arrows at dogs and cats trapped in orange crates; Carroll Edward Cole, who strangled a puppy as a child; Earl Shriner, who as a juvenile stuck firecrackers up the anuses of dogs; and Jeffrey Dahmer, who killed and impaled animals while a juvenile. Arkow concluded that the courts and social services should give serious attention to a triad of symptoms: cruelty to animals, physical abuse by one or both parents, and violence directed toward people.

An article by Crowell (1999) also focused on the responsibility factor. The author noted that social and behavioral science professionals have recognized the link between violence toward animals and violence committed upon, and by, children. Many jurisdictions, however, have been slow to respond to the connection legally. Crowell concluded that mandatory cross-reporting systems need to be implemented and that only through the combined efforts of agencies concerned with the prevention of animal and child abuse can such abuse be decreased.

Two recent articles focused on the contributions of law enforcement in the prevention of both domestic violence and animal cruelty. The first article, by Turner (2000), cited a 1995 study by Quinlisk of battered women in Wisconsin. This study found that in four out of five cases, abusive partners had also been violent toward pets or livestock. Furthermore, the women indicated that the abuse of the animals had been carried out in front of them and their children. Turner also cited the study by DeViney et al. (1983) that found that in 88 percent of families where children had been physically abused, there were also records of animal abuse. As a result of these studies, Turner recommended that officers and investigators responding to domestic violence calls or reports of animal abuse or neglect "consider the scene in its entirety" (Turner, 2000, p. 28). Turner also suggested that police departments work collaboratively with services for children and animal protection agencies in their communities because many battered women are reluctant to leave an abusive situation if they must leave their pets behind. Turner noted that animal shelters serve a critical function in that many shelters have contingencies to temporarily house the pets of battered women. Turner concluded by urging police departments to work closely with battered women's shelters and animal protection agencies to enhance victim services.

In a second article, by Ponder and Lockwood (2000), the authors report that the Baltimore Police Department receives approximately 64,000 domestic–violence-related calls each year. Ponder and Lockwood reported that Col. Margaret Patten, head of the department's domestic violence program, upon learning of the connection between domestic violence and animal abuse, initiated an outreach campaign targeting various community resources. Patten's goal was to educate representatives from schools, hospitals, child protection services, and other community agencies about domestic abuse.

The authors cited a second example of law enforcement's efforts to help prevent both domestic violence and animal abuse. Chief Roger Beaupre of Biddeford, Maine, received federal funding to start a domestic violence task force to help prevent both domestic violence and animal cruelty. After citing some further examples of successful prevention programs focusing on the link between domestic violence and animal cruelty, the authors concluded that much can be gained by implementing multidisciplinary programs to prevent family violence and animal cruelty (Ponder & Lockwood, 2000).

Commentary on the Literature

The review of the literature reveals that the relationship of cruelty to animals to human violence has been studied in various contexts. Some of the studies have concluded that cruelty to animals is a viable predictor of later human violence, while others have concluded it is an insignificant or a confounding factor. Although the literature remains inconclusive as to the exact relationship of cruelty to animals and violence committed against humans, some studies (e.g., Ressler et al., 1998) offer compelling evidence that cruelty to animals can offer insights into the complex phenomenon of interpersonal violence. These studies further suggest that cruelty to animals might be a precursor to potentially analogous behavior directed against humans.

The review of the literature provides a thematic summary of the literature to date. It is evident that many factors must be examined in tandem in order for the correlation between cruelty to animals and later violence against humans to offer significant meaning within the context of human behavior, particularly behavior involving interpersonal violence. The literature examined the correlation from various theoretical and applied perspectives.

Factors such as gender, race, place of residence, social class, and employment status were not key issues in the studies cited. The subjects in most of the studies, other than those focusing on victims of domestic violence, were adolescent males, an expected factor given the studies' focus on aggressive behavior. Exceptions to an all-male population sampling were the study by MacDonald (1963), which included subjects of both genders; the study by Lewis et al. (1983), which included both male and female children ages three through twelve; the study by DeViney et al. (1983), which included adults and juveniles of both genders; the study by Achenbach (1991), which included both boys and girls, ages four through sixteen; and the study by Miller and Knutson (1997), which included university students of both genders. Social class and employment status were distinguished only in the studies by Climent et al. (1972) and Luk et al. (1999). Climent et al. distinguished criteria with respect to age, sex, race, and place of residence in an effort to match controls. Luk et al. included demographic data for the parents of the children studied. The authors also distinguished the criteria of age, sex, race, and place of residence in an effort to match controls.

Three of the studies were conducted outside the United States. The study by Youssef et al. (1999) was conducted in Egypt; the study by Santtila and Haapasalo (1997) was conducted in Finland; and the study by Vermuelen and Odendaal (1993), cited in chapter 1, was conducted in South Africa. The diverse geographical locations of these studies underscore that cruelty is a cross-cultural concern.

Lockwood and Church (1998), Ressler et al. (1998), and Hellman and Blackman (1966) examined the correlation of animal cruelty and violence toward people in terms of its predictive potential. (Ressler et al. also measured other variables, such as firesetting and cruelty against children, and Hellman and Blackman focused on cruelty to animals within the context of the triad.) These studies also implied that the correlation might be applicable as a means to facilitate violence prevention and intervention. However, the successful application of any theory requires first that the theoretical concepts involved be precisely articulated and defined. Kellert and Felthous (1985) and Heide (1992) rigorously defined the factors relevant to their respective studies and established standards for future studies. Clearly, theoretical rigor and practical application are interdependent, and the exclusion of either seriously compromises the validity and value of any given study. For example, in addition to having verification problems, the study by Climent et al. (1972) failed to adequately and meaningfully operationalize variables with respect to violence. Likewise, the study by Miller and Knutson (1997) failed to clearly define cruelty to animals. What is not clearly defined cannot be reliably measured.

A valid and meaningful analysis of the correlation is not possible unless and until the variables in the inquiry are appropriately defined and understood. Owens and Straus (1975), among others, also supported the need for precise definition. Keeney and Heide (1995) provided, as their expressed goal, a clearer definition of the serial killer, the type of violent offender most often cited as having the symptom of cruelty to animals operative in the killer's juvenile history. Likewise, Vermeulen and Odendaal (1993) provided a clearly articulated typology of the phenomenon of cruelty to animals. The authors determined that a lack of standardized definitions concerning companion animal abuse had impeded research and the reporting of abuse.

Kellert and Felthous (1985) presented a systematic framework to examine the phenomenon of cruelty to animals and its relationship to human violence. Their specifics of act and motive provide clear and meaningful parameters within which the phenomenon of cruelty to animals might be articulated and understood. These authors also introduced the concept of frequency with respect to acts of cruelty committed and emphasized its importance. They determined that frequency was a significant factor because it indicated a pattern of escalating violent behavior that was crucial to the correlation. Within this framework, a random act of investigative or experimental animal cruelty is distinct from a pattern of behavior.

An isolated behavior that is clearly tied to a child's curiosity, such as Jeffrey Dahmer's childhood fascination with roadkill or the dissection of a fish to see what is inside, can be clearly distinguished from a pattern of escalating frequency and severity of acts that was indeed in Dahmer's background. In Dahmer's case, a fascination with roadkill and the dissection of fish and frogs escalated to include the torturing and killing of cats and dogs and, ultimately, human beings. In addition, Dahmer experimented on dogs and cats to practice the same preservation techniques he would eventually use on his human victims. Dahmer's case therefore demonstrates not only a continuum of childhood cruelty to animals and later violence against humans but also a continuum in kind. Dahmer's case would appear to support the view that the only way to test the validity of a significant relationship between cruelty to animals and later violence against humans is to pursue the hypothesis with rigorous clarity of meaning and motive.

The study by Owens and Straus (1975) also focused on the concept of a continuum of violence. Their research demonstrated a continuum of violence beginning in childhood and continuing into adulthood. Although the study did not address cruelty to animals, it is suggested here that if a correlation between cruelty to animals and interpersonal violence is conclusively demonstrated, then the broad implications of Owens and Straus's research would be applicable to violence against animals as well as to violence directed against humans. In this study, a relationship was substantiated between childhood exposure to violence and a tolerance for interpersonal violence, including political violence, in adulthood.

The concept of a continuum was also addressed by Arluke et al. (1999) in terms of a violence graduation hypothesis. Although the authors' findings did not support the graduation hypothesis, the authors suggested that a confounding factor might have been the fact that their study was based on reports of single acts of cruelty committed. The authors concluded that if frequency of acts of animal cruelty had been measured, the graduation hypothesis might have been supported.

Similarly, Hickey (2002) suggested that if proper definitions and measurements were used, the graduation hypothesis would be supported. According to the author, a viable "etiology of animal abuse" must first be established in order to understand the role that cruelty to animals plays in homicidal aggression (p. 100). As an example of methodological saliency, Hickey referred to the nine motivations for childhood mistreatment of animals established by Kellert and Felthous. The author concluded that without proper intervention, children may indeed graduate to more serious abuses, including crimes against people. Research by Wright and Hensley (2003) provided preliminary support for the violence graduation hypothesis in a sample of five serial killers.

The need for precision of definition is not restricted to the phenomenon of cruelty to animals. Indeed, enhanced understanding and definition of *criminal* versus *violent* behavior must be furthered. Climent et al. (1972) concluded that criminal behavior was related to cultural factors whereas violent behavior was related to individual factors. Clearly, criminal behavior is not always manifested as violent behavior. Therefore, greater attention should be given to both forms of behavior in order to attain better insight as to why many criminals do not cross the line into violent behavior.

Extrapolating from the literature focusing on serial or predatory offenders, such as Ressler et al. (1998) and Norris (1988), a concept begins to emerge of an offender who has experienced extreme childhood violence, whether or not involving cruelty to animals, and has as a result developed a high tolerance and acceptance of violence as a way to reconcile conflict. In addition, the severity of this exposure to violence has nurtured antisocial impulses. The offender, while clearly able to distinguish wrong from right, on the basis of individual factors, is compelled to act on these antisocial impulses. This type of offender is psychopathic and *deliberate*. Unlike the mentally ill offender whose illness impedes his or her ability to fully understand and bear responsibility for the actions committed, the psychopath controls, tortures, and kills precisely because he knows what he is doing. According to Norris, "the very dark behavior of the serial killer is often masked by a veneer of a very good and socially rewarded behavior" (p. 226). Norris cited John Wayne Gacy and Ted Bundy as two classic examples of this type of offender (pp. 228–229). Likewise, the description of the serial offender offered by Keeney and Heide (1993) as the "next-door neighbor" hints at the insidious nature of this type of offender. Often appearing to be perfectly normal, the serial killer might live among the rest of us without our knowing. As described by Schechter and Everitt (1996), the serial killer might even be charming in appearance and demeanor and appear to be on the path to a bright political future, such as Ted Bundy was. Bundy's persona hints at the problematic nature of violence.

Let us return for a moment to the conclusion reached by Felthous and Kellert (1987) that inconclusive findings with respect to the correlation were often the result of inadequate definition of the variables and/or a lack of thoroughness in the methodologies used. It might be suggested that the authors' conclusion be taken a step further. That is, methodologies and definitions aside, it might be equally important to ask the right questions of the right subjects. In other words, the fact that a given study may not have substantiated the significance of the correlation does not necessarily indicate that the correlation does not exist.

A number of the studies involved subjects within a hospital psychiatric setting, such as MacDonald's landmark study (1963). Further research is necessary with respect to the phenomenon of cruelty to animals as it is perpetrated by the mentally ill when compared to normal populations. There are two reasons for this recommendation. The first reason is of *theoretical* importance, and it is based on the fact that extreme cruelty to animals is considered by many individuals (including law enforcement officials, animal welfare officials, educators and school counselors, and youth and family service providers) to be the manifestation of a psychiatric disorder of one form or another, rather than a conscious act committed by a mentally competent person. In this view, cruelty to animals is explained as a *pathological* rather than a *purposeful* act. This distinction is important because in the first instance (pathology), cruelty to animals is viewed as the incidental manifestation of an illness rather than as the primary and conscious will to hurt or kill (purpose). This distinction is critical in view of the fact that Kellert and Felthous (1995) determined that the type of cruelty to animals that was relevant to the correlation was *deliberate* cruelty. Therefore, substantiation by further research that sociopathy, psychopathy, or antisocial personality (essentially interchangeable terms) is correlated with at least some forms of animal cruelty would have strong ramifications for intervention and public policy considerations.

The second reason that an understanding of mental status is important with respect to the correlation follows logically from the first and is of *practical* importance. If further research validates the sociopathic impetus for some forms of animal cruelty, then this finding would reinforce typologies such as that of the serial killer and would affect the way that both law enforcement and the judicial system apply justice to such offenders. This finding would also have broad implications for the assessment and treatment of the mentally ill who have committed acts of cruelty to animals. The "further research" advocated here of course requires methodological rigor and precise definitions as exemplified by Kellert and Felthous (1985) and Heide (1992).

The issue of deliberate cruelty is critical in view of the literature addressing serial and predatory killers. Most often, the serial killer is described as a deliberate killer. The literature has often indicated that cruelty to animals is frequently a component of the serial killer's behavioral history. In fact, MacDonald himself alluded to this issue when he concluded "that the triad was not a favorable prognostic factor in those who had threatened homicide" because psychiatric patients often express delusional threats of anger and violence without ever carrying them out. In this context, the outcome of MacDonald's study makes perfect sense. Delusional patients, who made up a good portion of MacDonald's sample (thirty-five out of one hundred), might not have been an appropriate group with which to test the relationship between the triad and later violence.

One might argue, conversely, that MacDonald's study might well have served to strengthen the validity of the correlation. This assertion might be especially true considering the fact that some of the researchers who have most strongly supported the validity of the correlation, such as Kellert and Felthous, have emphasized that the type of cruelty to animals that is relevant to the correlation must be deliberate. Ascione (1998b) noted that Felthous and Kellert defined "substantial cruelty to animals" as a "pattern of deliberately, repeatedly, and unnecessarily hurting of vertebrate animals in a manner likely to cause serious injury," whereas Brown defined cruelty as "unnecessary suffering knowingly inflicted on a sentient being (animal or human)" (p. 85).

Returning to MacDonald's conclusion that the triad was not significant in the case of subjects who *threatened* violence, it is suggested here that MacDonald's findings make logical sense because the kind of cruelty to animals that the correlation is concerned with is deliberate cruelty committed by a perpetrator who knows what he is doing. Considering the importance placed on intentional acts of cruelty, any cruelty to animals that is committed by a mentally ill individual may be more a component of that individual's particular pathology than a symptom that is relevant to the correlation. Heller et al. (1984) reached this conclusion when they reported that the presence of the triad in the history of an offender indicates "strong antisocial impulses inadequately controlled rather than psychotic tendencies toward criminal behavior" (p. 153). It is such antisocial impulses that have prompted the FBI's Behavioral Sciences Unit to develop the profile of the serial killer, a profile that most often includes cruelty to animals.

The importance of the suggested relationship of cruelty to animals and the profile of the serial killer is twofold. First, those who support the validity of the correlation postulate that it can serve as a useful tool in helping solve these most difficult cases. Holmes and De Burger (1988) estimated that between 3,500 and 5,000 victims are killed by serial killers each year in the United States (pp. 19–20).

Criminal profiling has been somewhat helpful in identifying and capturing killers. It has demonstrated that an accurate understanding of the developmental background of the serial killer is essential. The past history of the offender directly serves to facilitate the future identification of the offender. Indeed, the serial killer's past may be the only viable link to his eventual capture. Just as it has been suggested that the development of the serial killer is a continuum of escalating anger and violence, the methodology of his apprehension may also be a continuum. If cruelty to animals is conclusively determined by the research to be significant to later human violence, its potentially vital role in this continuum of escalating violence will be established.

Extrapolating from the study by Climent et al. (1972), it might be suggested that the serial killer's extreme form of violent behavior is the result of individual factors. However, if, as Climent et al. suggested, criminal behavior is the result of cultural factors, then sobering implications might be drawn concerning culture and its unique ability to tolerate or condemn violence. In this view, the animal cruelty that was reported by Grandin (1988) with respect to factory farming might suggest disconcerting implications. For example, the question arises as to whether acts of animal cruelty committed within a socially accepted institutionalized setting are tied to cultural or individual factors. Regardless of individual views as to the ethics of eating the flesh of animals, factory farming is a culturally and legally sanctioned form of violence against animals that, according to Mason and Singer (1990), affects billions of animals in the United States each year. And considering the high incidence of cruelty to animals reported by Grandin at slaughter plants and auction markets, does the cultural institution of factory farming increase our tolerance for violence overall? It might be argued that this question, posed within the context of the findings of Owens and Straus, encourages further inquiry.

In summary, it would appear that regardless of the factors that motivate or tolerate cruelty to animals in our society, effective screening instruments and intervention strategies must be developed. Guymer et al. (2001) developed an instrument that distinguishes children who perpetuate malicious acts of cruelty and warrant clinical intervention from children who commit typical acts of animal cruelty and do not need mental health treatment. Quinlisk (1999) and Lewchanin and Zimmerman (2000) developed manuals to assist mental health clinicians in assessing children referred for animal cruelty. Clearly effective intervention, as well as prevention of animal cruelty, must be orchestrated by a coalition of a community's diverse professional resources (Arluke & Lockwood, 1997; Ascione, 1997, 2001; Crowell, 1999; Ponder & Lockwood, 2000; Turner, 2000). Lewchanin and Zimmerman, for example, included police, child protective workers, mental health and health care professionals, clergy, and animal control and humane officers as necessary participants in this process. Arkow (1998) and Quinlisk (1999) both placed special emphasis on the role of veterinarians as a vital link in the prevention and intervention of animal abuse.

Perhaps Cazaux (1999) best encapsulated implications for further study. Cazaux concluded that it was time to bring cruelty to animals into the criminological fold. The author expressed concern with respect to both cultural and individual manifestations of animal cruelty. Referring to culture-based animal cruelty, Cazaux concluded that the "criminological arena must not ignore these large scale systems of animal abuse" (p. 118). Likewise, Lockwood (1999) concluded that the increasing societal awareness of the role of cruelty to animals "in the much broader universe of antisocial and criminal behavior is an important step on the path to a truly humane society" (p. 7). In the next chapter, we draw from the research literature to construct theoretical explanations why some individuals initially abuse animals and later advance to hurting human beings.

THREE THEORIES OF OFFENDERS

This chapter proposes three theories that explain the link between animal cruelty in childhood and later violence towards humans. Two theories, the Displaced Aggression Theory and the Sadistic Theory, have been constructed by extrapolating from the seven motives presented by Kellert and Felthous that appear to have particular significance for the correlation between animal cruelty and subsequent violence toward humans. The third theory, the Sexually Polymorphous Theory, is based on the findings of Wax and Haddox. These theories and the offender types based on them are not mutually exclusive. Rather, they are constructed to provide insights into the dominant influences and distinctive attributes particular to each. These theories will later be examined in terms of sample subjects who appear to represent each of the offender types.

Displaced Aggression Theory

The Displaced Aggression Theory posits that individuals hurt animals and people to demonstrate control and to express anger that is removed, or "displaced," from its original source. This theory is constructed from four of the seven motives presented by Kellert and Felthous (1985) that are deemed to be significant with respect to the correlation between childhood animal cruelty and subsequent human violence. These four motives are:

1. To control an animal.

2. To express aggression through an animal.

3. To retaliate against another person.

4. Displacement of hostility from a person to an animal.

Jeffrey Dahmer, a serial killer whose life and crimes have been well documented, appears to serve as a good example of the Displaced Aggression Theory offender. Dahmer was ultimately sentenced to fifteen consecutive life sentences. His high intelligence and articulateness provided insights into his thoughts and the driving forces behind his crimes. In 1994, he was beaten to death by a fellow inmate.

Dahmer reported to his probation officer, Donna Chester, that although he was never abused by his parents, his childhood was "not happy" (Davis, 1991, pp. 31–33). He described his feelings toward both parents as "mixed or neutral" (p. 32). Documents demonstrated that the Dahmer household was in turmoil. His parents divorced when Dahmer was eighteen. At that time, the parents' main concern appeared to be custody of his younger brother, David. In 1982, when Dahmer was twenty-two years old, his mother won a restraining order that prohibited her husband from "molesting or assaulting her or the minor children" (Dvorchak & Holewa, 1991, p. 37). Throughout much of his life, Dahmer reportedly felt alienated and rejected and longed to be noticed and accepted by his parents (Davis, 1991). According to Hellman and Blackman (1966), the rejection of a parent is a very significant and painful experience that might lead to aggression.

Dahmer's childhood fascination with death and his propensity for collecting roadkill and dissecting small animals have already been noted. As a teenager, he targeted larger animals, including dogs. The remains of a dog, presumably killed by Dahmer, were found by a neighbor in the woods behind Dahmer's house (Baumann, 1991). The severed head of the dog was impaled on a sharp stick, and the rest of its mutilated remains were found nailed to a nearby tree. Dahmer reportedly used animals to practice the techniques that he would later use on his human victims. According to his stepmother, Dahmer "would take animals and melt them down to the bone" (p. 94). Years later, Dahmer explained to the police how he boiled the head of one of his victims, Anthony Sears, "in order to remove the skin" (p. 108). During Dahmer's trial, the prosecuting attorney, E. Michael McCann, argued that Dahmer's need to control resulted in the crude brain surgeries that he sometimes performed on his victims in the hope that he would create zombies who would serve as his sexual slaves (Dvorchak & Holewa, 1991).

Dahmer's mental state was debated by psychiatrists. The issue of psychopathic versus psychotic behavior was discussed earlier with respect to the study by MacDonald (1963) that addressed the relationship between the triad and the threat to kill. MacDonald reported that psychotic patients often experienced delusions of great anger that were never carried out. Dahmer's outward behavior was not delusional and was neither wild nor bizarre. In his dealings with others, Dahmer appeared to be cool and articulate to the point that he was able to convince three police officers that one of his victims, who had momentarily escaped, should be "returned to his care" (Baumann, 1991, p. 234).

Dr. Ashok Bedi, who had studied Dahmer's case file, concluded that the recurring theme in Dahmer's life was abandonment and that Dahmer's family had failed to provide him "with an infrastructure that would support him" (Dvorchak & Holewa, 1991, p. 142). The circumstances surrounding Dahmer's murder of Jeremiah Weinberger appear to support Bedi's assessment. Dahmer reported that after meeting Weinberger at a gay bar, the two returned to Dahmer's apartment, where they had sex. The next day, Weinberger expressed a desire to leave. Dahmer reported that he offered Weinberger a drink with a sleeping potion in it because he did not want to be alone. Dahmer said that he then strangled and dismembered Weinberger.

In conclusion, on the basis of the Displaced Aggression Theory, Dahmer is described as an individual who harbored a great deal of anger about his unhappy childhood and the parental rejection he experienced. Considering the loneliness that Dahmer's homosexuality engendered in him, some of this anger may have been self-directed. According to psychiatrist Dr. Gerson Kaplan, "the gruesome butchering of his homosexual partners can be understood as his way of trying to punish and deny that part of himself that he hated" (Baumann, 1991, p. 232). Some of the mutilations that he later performed on his human victims may have evolved directly from his fascination with death that originated in childhood. In this view, Dahmer's roadkill collections and animal dissections were the beginning of a continuum. Ultimately, Dahmer's unreconciled anger toward his parents, compounded by his need to control, compelled his escalating violence that began with animals and culminated in serial murder.

Sadistic Theory

The Sadistic Theory posits that individuals hurt animals and people because they find these activities pleasurable in themselves and/or they enjoy the shocked, terrified, or horrified reactions of the victims or other audiences. This theory is extrapolated from the remaining two of the seven motives presented by Kellert and Felthous that are believed to be relevant to the correlation. The ninth of Kellert and Felthous's (1985) motives is "nonspecific sadism." They report that "the act of killing was often associated in these cases with satisfying a pleasurable impulse, and extinguishing a life became a primary objective unrelated to any fear or hatred of the animal" (p. 1124). Their sixth motive, to shock people for amusement, is also a dynamic operative in the Sadistic Theory offender.

This theory is exemplified by Leonard Lake, a serial offender whom Norris describes as exhibiting "unusual cruelty to animals" (1988, p. 155). Lake and his companion, Charles Ng, tortured and filmed their victims. Leonard tortured his female victims with sadomasochistic devices that forced them to scream out in pain. He served as a Marine in Vietnam and later murdered his best friend from his Vietnam years, Charles Gunnar. He also murdered his younger brother, Donald, who visited him at his survivalist compound in California. He was never convicted of any of his crimes, however, because he committed suicide upon his arrest in San Francisco by taking a cyanide pill that he carried with him.

Lake fantasized that, in a post–nuclear-holocaust civilization, women would serve him. He established a survivalist camp in California called the Mother Lode and later drifted to varying locations. He committed a series of murders; his former wife, Cricket Balazs, often served as a fence for the goods and credit cards that he stole. Lake often assumed the identities of his male victims; a cache of stolen vehicle registrations, driver's licenses, and credit cards were found in his last residence, a cabin in the Blue Ridge Mountains.

Balazs reportedly assisted Lake in making pornographic films, including custom sadomasochistic tapes, which Lake created for a variety of clients. Lake scripted, directed, and filmed these tapes. Balazs suspected correctly, however, that he was "making even weirder violence and pornography videos on the side" (Norris, 1988, p. 156).

Lake's private films were doubtless made to further dehumanize and torture his victims. Lake taunted his victims while they were being filmed. Apparently, these films were also made for the shock they would engender upon their viewing. The police who discovered the videos were reportedly horrified by their content (Norris, 1988).

The Sadistic Theory offender, such as Lake, takes great pleasure in the process of death. In this regard, some would argue that he differed significantly from Dahmer in that Dahmer first drugged, and only then strangled, his victims. According to his defense attorneys, the act of killing was incidental to Dahmer's crimes and Dahmer "did not like killing" (Schwartz, 1992, p. 206). One expert witness who testified at Dahmer's trial, Dr. Judith Becker, described Dahmer as "obsessed by necrophilia" (p. 204). Dahmer killed his victims as a means to an end. Discussion of this apparent qualitative difference between Lake's and Dahmer's crimes is not intended to minimize the suffering of Dahmer's victims. Dahmer's only surviving victim, Tracy Edwards, reported to the police upon his escape that Dahmer had threatened to cut out and eat his heart (Dvorchak & Holewa, 1991, p. 2). Some might have interpreted this threat as the result of Dahmer's frustration and anger at having lost control of the situation, rather than as evidence that Dahmer killed because he took pleasure in the killing. Both Lake and Dahmer left many victims in their wake.

In summary, the Sadistic Theory offender clearly kills with pleasure and enjoys the control that he is able to exert over others. He is also able to control the process of his killing. He has the ability to take his time to maximize his victims' fear and pain. This type of offender enjoys his victims' suffering and derives pleasure from the shock and horror that his crimes engender in others.

Sexually Polymorphous Theory

The Sexually Polymorphous Theory posits that individuals hurt animals and people because these violent activities are necessary for them to achieve sexual pleasure and release. Wax and Haddox (1974c) focused on an analysis of sexually aberrant behavior, particularly from a developmental perspective. The authors explain that infantile sexuality assumes a number of forms (is polymorphous) and that the types of experiences sought in the expression of perverse sexual activities vary greatly in number and type. The aim is the reduction of the tension associated with sexual excitement.

"Perverse" sexual activity is a generalized term that is both individually and culturally subjective. The term as used here refers to sexual activities that are violent and outside the parameters of social norms. The offender fitting this category exhibits a fusion of sexual and aggressive behavior. According to Wax and Haddox, this type of offender must commit violence to achieve sexual release. Excessive cruelty to animals provided the necessary release in the six cases studied by the authors. In all six cases, however, violence against humans occurred in various forms, including rape and murder. This type of behavior has been frequently cited in the literature with respect to serial killers. The Federal Bureau of Investigation's (FBI) *Crime Classification Manual* lists three types of sexual homicide: organized, disorganized, and mixed (Douglas, Burgess, Burgess, & Ressler, 1997, pp. 123–136). This type of offender commits his periodic murders to satisfy a sexual urge.

In all six cases, the adolescents were products of "chaotic households and victims of irregular child-rearing approaches" (Wax & Haddox, 1974c, p. 105). Although the terms "chaotic household" and "irregular child-rearing approaches" are imprecise, family dysfunction of one kind or another is often reported in the literature on animal cruelty.

The study by Wax and Haddox was not gender-specific in its analysis of parental abuse. However, Norris notes that the FBI's Behavioral Sciences Unit "has discovered that the serial killer has a clear history of abuse and that he was the victim of considerable abuse as a child, usually by the mother" (1988, p. 93). Research shows that many of the most infamous serial killers on record, despite their varying typologies, share the common factor of childhood abuse by their mothers; such killers include Kenneth Bianchi, Ed Kemper, Henry Lee Lucas, Charles Manson, and Ed Gein.

The Sexually Polymorphous Theory offender is unique in that sexuality and aggression have become developmentally fused, and the two are mutually inclusive in the psyche of the offender. Henry Lee Lucas, a serial murderer who was convicted of eleven murders (Norris, 1988) and confessed to as many as 150 additional murders across the nation (Cox, 1991) is an example of this type of offender.

Lucas, by all accounts, was severely abused by his mother, Viola. In his own words, Lucas explained: "I was dressed like a girl by my mother. And I stayed that way for two or three years. And after that I was treated like what I call the dog of the family. I was beaten; I was made to do things that no human bein' would want to do" (Norris, 1988, p. 109).

Viola also abused Lucas's father, Anderson, an alcoholic who had lost both legs when, in a drunken stupor, he fell beneath a slow-moving train. Viola Lucas entertained a steady stream of sexual partners, and she had a live-in boyfriend who also abused the young Lucas (Norris, 1988).

On the night of January 11, 1960, Lucas murdered his mother. He was convicted of second-degree murder and sentenced to twenty to forty years in prison (Cox, 1991). He was paroled in 1970 because of over-crowding in the Michigan prison system (Norris, 1988).

Lucas went on to stay with various relatives, ultimately staying with his half-sister, Opal, and her husband, Kenneth Jennings. Upon Lucas's rearrest one year later for attempted kidnapping, his sister informed the police that she suspected that the arrest had to do "with the animals" (Cox, 1991, p. 64). She explained to the police that she and her husband had had a dog and a goat when Lucas moved in with them but that about one month before, the dog was found hanging by a rope in the shed and the goat was "all butchered up" (p. 64). Lucas was convicted of the kidnapping charges, for which he served three and a half years.

Upon his release, Lucas, often accompanied by his homosexual part-ner, Ottis Toole, reportedly began a killing spree that continued along the highways of the Southwest and into Florida. The spree came to an end in 1983 when Lucas was arrested in Texas on a weapons charge. Within weeks Lucas had confessed to the murder of his common-law wife, Becky Powell (Toole's sister), and hundreds of other victims. Although many of Lucas's confessions were proven to be false, it is probable that Lucas mur-dered scores, if not hundreds, of strangers, along Interstate 35 in Texas and in a number of neighboring states (Norris, 1988).

In-depth exploration of Lucas's life revealed that he had demon-strated an "escalating propensity toward violence" (Norris, 1988, p. 125). Lucas had been a fire starter and was "maliciously cruel to ani-mals" (p. 125). Lucas practiced bestiality as an older child. As a young teenager, he reported having sex with his half-brother and with the an-imals whose throats the two would cut open before performing bestial-ity. Lucas often caught small animals and skinned them alive for pleasure.

Lucas became involved in rape as an adolescent and a single murder as a young adult. He eventually became a serial killer, committing mul-tiple murders, necrophilia, torture, mutilation, dismemberment, and totemic preservation of the remains of his victims (Norris, 1988). Lucas "came alive" only in the death of another human being and gained sex-ual potency after he had bludgeoned and strangled his sex partner into a coma or death (Norris, 1988, p. 122). Consistent with the Sexually

Polymorphous Theory, Lucas reportedly killed to gain sexual potency because he was "unable to have sex with a living person" (p. 124).

The three theories of offenders are tentative and require further study. It is apparent, however, that Lucas's crimes differed significantly from those committed by *sadistic offenders*, such as Leonard Lake, and *displaced-aggression offenders*, such as Jeffrey Dahmer. Lake killed for a variety of reasons, including material gain. Even when his crimes were sexually oriented, they were committed with a control that was virtually choreographed. The proverbial sadist, Lake would often torture his victims for days. He and his wife shared not only sexual relations but also sadomasochistic tendencies. In this respect, Lake had the ability to compartmentalize his sadistic tendencies. He could pragmatically channel them into making movies for his clients' enjoyment and for his own monetary profit, or into murder. Lake committed some of his crimes with an accomplice, Charles Ng, within a mutually controlled environment. In contrast, Lucas's attacks were frenzied and finite. Unlike Dahmer, who was reportedly able to consummate consensual sexual relations with his victims prior to killing them, Lucas could achieve sexual release only by killing his victims. For Lucas, sexual release and killing were combined into a single act.

As noted earlier, the three types of offenders proposed here are not mutually exclusive. For example, Dvorchak and Holewa (1991) report that Dr. Ashok Bedi had concluded that Dahmer "showed a lot of confusion between sexuality and aggression" (p. 143). It can be argued that confusion between sexual and aggressive drives and the polymorphous combination of the two drives are separate phenomena. Ultimately, however, the primary motive of each of the three offender types is distinct and warrants separate classification. Kellert and Felthous (1985) concluded that motive was a critical factor in defining and understanding cruelty to animals. We propose that motive is equally important in understanding individuals who progress from hurting animals to hurting people.

The chapters in part I provide the foundation for the present study, which includes both quantitative and qualitative assessments. The empirical part of the study that tests the link between four types of animal cruelty committed in childhood and subsequent violence toward humans is the focus of part II. Case studies of subjects who moved from acts of animal cruelty to violence against people are used to illustrate the three theories of offenders in part III.

Part Two
ANIMAL CRUELTY AND SUBSEQUENT HUMAN VIOLENCE: AN EMPIRICAL INVESTIGATION

METHOD AND STUDY DESIGN

T his chapter describes the sample and data collection plan for the present study, then focuses on discussion of the variables. The variables measured in this study included extensive demographic and family background information about sample subjects and detailed information about animal cruelty that was committed and observed by the subjects (e.g., frequency, seriousness, subject's response, and circumstances surrounding the incident).

Subjects

The targeted sample sizes for this study were fifty violent and fifty non-violent offenders. Two lists of violent and nonviolent inmates were randomly generated by computer with the assistance of institutional staff located at a maximum-security prison in Florida. At the time of the study, this facility housed over a thousand inmates who were serving lengthy sentences based on the present offense and/or previous criminal history. The offenses for which offenders were presently incarcerated (i.e., the commitment or primary offenses) were used as the screening variable by institutional staff. Verification of nonviolent-offender status was made subsequently by the senior interviewer by checking case files for violent prior offenses and by inquiring about violent crimes during the interviews. Cases initially identified as nonviolent offenders who were found to have a history of criminal violence were eliminated from study participation at the time of discovery.

One hundred subjects, fifty violent offenders and fifty nonviolent offenders, were approached by the senior author for interviews in accordance with the random-generation lists for interviews.[1] Ninety-seven interviews were successfully completed with these one hundred inmates. Three of the violent offenders refused to continue during the interview process. Another two violent subjects were disqualified because serious mental health problems interfered with their ability to participate meaningfully in the research. Five of the nonviolent subjects were disqualified after the interviewer learned that the "nonviolent offender" had committed violent prior offenses. As a result of the three refusals and seven disqualifications, ninety subjects were included in the study: forty-five nonviolent and forty-five violent subjects.

The two groups were fairly similar to one another. As depicted in table 4.1, the median ages for the two groups were similar: 31.8 for nonviolent subjects and 32.3 for violent subjects. We compared violent and nonviolent offenders on four demographic variables: race (white/nonwhite), education (high school graduate/not high school graduate), marital status (married/not married), and children (none/one or more). We chose chi-square as our test statistic for these analyses and those that follow because we are using dichotomous data.[2] Statistical significance was not revealed with respect to race (chi-square = 3.629; d.f. = 1; p = .058), but the .05 level borders the level of significance (p < .05). More violent (56 percent) than nonviolent subjects (36 percent) were white.

Significance was not revealed with respect to education when the two groups were compared (chi-square = 3.242; d.f. = 1; p = .072). The .07 level, however, demonstrates a tendency toward significance. A greater proportion of violent subjects (55 percent) than nonviolent subjects (36 percent) had completed a high school education or its equivalent.

As also shown in table 4.1, significance was not revealed when the two groups of subjects were compared with respect to either marital status (chi-square = 2.248; d.f. = 1; p = .134) or the subjects' known number of children (chi-square = .382; d.f. = 1; p = .536). A greater proportion of nonviolent subjects (20 percent) than violent subjects (9 percent) reported that they were married. The proportions of nonviolent and violent subjects who reported no known children were similar: 72 percent of violent subjects compared to 66 percent of nonviolent subjects.

Qualitative summaries of both the subjects' instant and most serious committed offenses are depicted in tables 4.2 through 4.5.

Table 4.1. Quantitative Summary of Subjects' Demographic and Personal Data

Variable	% Nonviolent**	N	% Violent**	N	Chi-Square Results
Median Age in Years	31.8		32.3		
Race					
White	36		56		
Nonwhite	64	45	44	45	*3.629; d.f. = 1; p = .058 (ns)
Education					
High School					
Grad/GED	36		55		
Non-High School	64	45	45	44	3.242; d.f. = 1; p = .072 (ns)
Marital Status					
Married	20		9		
Not Married	80	45	91	45	2.248; d.f. = 1; p = .134 (ns)
# Known Children					
None	66		72		
One or More	34	41	28	43	.382; d.f. = 1; p = .536 (ns)

*Note: Not significant but demonstrates a tendency toward significance.
**Values, other than age, are in percentages.

Table 4.2. Qualitative Summary of Subjects' Instant Offenses/ Nonviolent Offenders (in real numbers)

Offense Type	Number of Nonviolent Offenders
Constructive Possession	3
Obtain Lodging/Intent to Fraud	1
Trafficking in Stolen Property	1
Grand Theft $300 < $20,000	1
Grand Theft Motor Vehicle	1
Acquire Property/Racketeer	4
Cocaine—Sale or Purchase	5
Cocaine—Sale/Manufacture/Delivery	3
Trafficking in Cocaine	2
Trafficking in Cocaine/400G-U/150KG	2
Sell/Purchase Cocaine/Heroin/within 1000 ft. School	1
Transmit Contraband within Prison (drugs)	2
Introduction of Drugs into Correctional Facility	1
Escape	1
Possession of a Firearm by a Felon	2
Burglary of an Unoccupied Structure or Conveyance	7
Burglary/Armed of Unoccupied Structure	8
N	45

Table 4.3. Qualitative Summary of Subjects' Instant Offenses/Violent Offenders (in real numbers)

Offense Type	Number of Violent Offenders
Cocaine Possession	1
Trafficking in Stolen Property	1
Burglary of Occupied Dwelling	3
Armed Burglary	1
Robbery with Firearm/Dangerous Weapon	3
Resisting a Law Enforcement Officer with Violence	1
Aggravated Assault of a Law Enforcement Officer	2
Kidnapping to Commit or Facilitate a Felony	1
Kidnapping/Assault or Terrorize	1
Aggravated Battery with Intended Harm	1
Attempted Sexual Battery with a Deadly Weapon	2
Aggravated Battery with a Deadly Weapon	1
Attempted Sexual Battery on a Child Under 12	1
Sexual Battery by an Adult on a Child Under 12	4
Sexual Battery with Physical Force	3
Sexual Battery/ Threat with a Deadly Weapon	4
Attempted Murder/3 Degree	1
DUI Manslaughter	1
2 Degree Murder in Commission of Dangerous Act	3
2 Degree Murder in Commission of a Felony	3
1 Degree Murder	7
N	45

Nonviolent offenses included crimes against property (including such offenses as grand theft, racketeering, and unoccupied burglary), drug-related offenses, and, in two instances, possession of a firearm by a felon (the firearm had not been used in the commission of any crime). As enumerated in table 4.2, with respect to the nonviolent subjects' instant offenses overall, 33 percent of the offenses involved unoccupied burglary, 24 percent involved other property crimes, and 36 percent involved drug-related offenses. The remaining 7 percent involved such offenses as escape and possession of a firearm by a felon. As delineated in table 4.3, violent offenses included crimes against the person such as assault, rape, and murder. With respect to the violent subjects' instant offenses overall, 33 percent included attempted murder, manslaughter, and murder; 31 percent involved sexual battery; and 11 percent involved aggravated battery, aggravated assault on a law enforcement officer, or resisting arrest with violence. The remaining instant offenses

Table 4.4. Qualitative Summary of Subjects' Most Serious Committed Offenses/Nonviolent Offenders (in real numbers)

Offense Type	Number of Nonviolent Offenders
Constructive Possession	2
Trafficking in Stolen Property	1
Grand Theft $300 < $20,000	1
Grand Theft Motor Vehicle	2
Acquire Property/Racketeer	4
Cocaine—Sale or Purchase	6
Cocaine—Sale/Manufacture/Delivery	2
Trafficking in Cocaine	2
Trafficking in Cocaine/400G-U/150KG	1
Sell/Purchase Cocaine/Heroin/within 1000 ft. School	1
Transmit Contraband (drugs) within Prison	2
Introduction of Drugs into Correctional Facility	1
Possession of a Firearm by a Felon	1
Burglary of an Unoccupied Structure or Conveyance	8
Burglary/Armed of Unoccupied Structure	9
N	43*

*Note: In two cases, files were screened to assure that only nonviolent offenses had been committed by the subjects. However, the most serious offenses were not recorded.

included such offenses as kidnapping, armed robbery, and offenses with a potential for violence (armed burglary, burglary of an occupied dwelling). Two offenders with violent commitment histories were presently incarcerated for nonviolent crimes, specifically, cocaine possession and trafficking in stolen property.

As depicted in table 4.4, the most serious offenses committed by nonviolent subjects demonstrate a similar pattern to that of the instant offenses. With the exception of one offense of possession of a firearm by a felon, all of the most serious offenses involved property crimes (63 percent) and drug-related offenses (35 percent).

As depicted in table 4.5, all of the most serious offenses committed by violent offenders reflect violent crimes. The majority of the offenses were murder or attempted murder (35 percent) and sex offenses (30 percent). Other offenses included assault and/or battery (19 percent), burglary of an occupied dwelling and armed burglary (9 percent), robbery with a dangerous weapon or firearm (5 percent), and resisting a law enforcement officer with violence (2 percent).

Table 4.5. Qualitative Summary of Subjects' Most Serious Committed Offenses/ Violent Offenders (in real numbers)

Offense Type	Number of Violent Offenders
Burglary of Occupied Dwelling	3
Armed Burglary	1
Robbery with Firearm or Dangerous Weapon	2
Resisting a Law Enforcement Officer with Violence	1
Aggravated Assault	1
Aggravated Assault of a Law Enforcement Officer	3
Aggravated Assault with Intent to Commit Felony	1
Aggravated Battery with a Deadly Weapon	1
Aggravated Battery with Intended Harm	2
Attempted Sexual Battery with a Deadly Weapon	1
Attempted Sexual Battery on a Child Under 12	1
Sexual Battery by Adult on a Child Under 12	4
Sexual Battery with Physical Force	3
Sexual Battery/Threat with a Deadly Weapon	4
Attempted Murder/3 Degree	1
2 Degree Murder in Commission of Dangerous Act	4
2 Degree Murder in Commission of a Felony	3
1 Degree Murder	7
N	43*

*Note: In two cases, most serious committed offense information was unavailable.

Data Collection Plan

Upon completion of coding, the data were entered into the SPSS program and a full range of statistical analyses was completed. Hypotheses were tested by chi-square analyses with the level of significance being set at the .05 level. Owing to the small number of cases with respect to some of the variables included in this study, variables were at times recoded in order to permit chi-square analyses. In other cases, qualitative analyses were conducted.

Instruments and Interview

Two data collection instruments were used in the survey. The Survivors' Coping Strategies (SCS) instrument (Heide, 1999), developed by Kathleen M. Heide and Eldra P. Solomon, was used to gather personal background data about the subjects. It contains 246 questions with respect to such issues as marital status, number of children, education, types of child abuse, child neglect, familial dysfunction, and substance abuse. The Children and Animals Assessment Instrument (CAAI) (Ascione, 1993; Ascione, Thompson, & Black, 1997), developed by Frank R. Ascione, was used to gather data on the subjects' experience with animals, including cruelty to animals either committed or observed by the subjects.

The two data collection instruments were used in face-to-face interviews conducted by the senior author. Many of the questions elicited extended discussion on the part of the subjects. A significant amount of qualitative as well as quantitative information was obtained in the interviews, which lasted from 45 minutes to 2.5 hours.

The CAAI instrument addresses animal issues by dividing animals into four categories: wild, farm, pet, and stray. The same questions are asked in each category. The survey, which was designed to administer to children, compensated for the varying educational levels of the subjects, which ranged from no formal education to doctoral-level work. In many cases, the questions invite extended dialogue, and, by virtue of their repetitive design, they provide time for the subjects to reflect and return to a category if desired. This process likely allowed for greater thoroughness of the information obtained than might have otherwise been the case.

The SCS instrument, by virtue of its extensive scope, facilitates the gathering of substantial background information. It provided a vehicle for the subjects to recall, and in many instances to reflect on, their lives and past experiences. The SCS instrument, which was administered first, provided a tie with the subjects' pasts that, in many cases, set the stage for enhanced recall and an inclination to share information during the administering of the CAAI instrument. Therefore, in many instances, the two surveys operated in tandem to provide substantial data about the subjects.

Data Collection Procedures

Approval for the study was granted by the Human Subjects Review Committee of the University of South Florida and by the Research Review Committee of the Florida Department of Corrections. The interview process began in July 1995 and concluded in April 1996. The nature of the study was explained to all of the selected subjects in individual interviews. The subjects were advised at this time that their participation was strictly voluntary and that if they agreed to participate, they could refuse to continue the interview at any time. The subjects were informed that they could refuse to answer any questions that made them feel uncomfortable or which they deemed in any way to be inappropriate. They were advised that the interviews would be taped and identified by a number assigned to them to facilitate interrater reliability. They were informed, however, that their right to privacy would be safeguarded and that their responses would not be tied to them in any way at any future date.

The interviews were conducted face-to-face. Prison officials were nearby but were not present during the interviews. The resulting privacy facilitated the interview process and the thoroughness with which it was conducted. Many of the interviews exceeded one hour, and some exceeded two hours in duration.

Reliability and Validity

To check reliability, 20 percent of the coded interviews ($N = 20$) were coded by a second coder after training. The 198 variables relative to the study were clearly articulated and operationalized and fully explained to the second coder prior to his rating of the cases. A comparison of the two sets of coded interviews demonstrated a reliability of 99 percent. The 1 percent difference resulted from coding variations in two instances. In one instance, the second coder reported that he presumed that empathy would be irrelevant to an act of cruelty concerning a snake, because he, like many individuals, was afraid of snakes. He reported that some snakes are highly dangerous and most individuals cannot tell poisonous from nonpoisonous snakes. Therefore, he assumed that aggressive behavior toward snakes was not cruel but rather a manifestation of a justified fear. After explaining to the second coder that the empathy variable was to be applied with respect to all species, this coding variation was reconciled.

In the second instance, the second coder had originally determined that the abuse against the subject in question was committed only by the stepfather, rather than by both the stepfather and the subject's natural mother. Upon reviewing the tape of the interview, however, the second coder agreed that both parental figures were abusers.

Measurements of the Variables

The code book used in this study consisted of 198 variables and was designed to correlate with the interview instruments and with the literature with respect to cruelty to animals and later violence against humans. Variables were designed to extrapolate comprehensive quantitative and qualitative data about the subjects' histories. The included variables were extrapolated from the Heide and Solomon instrument and addressed demographic and personal background issues, such as the subjects' criminal history, race, educational and marital status, and substance use. Variables were also designed with respect to the subjects' familial background, including substance abuse by parental figures, abuse against the subject, and familial dysfunction. The variables pertaining to cruelty to animals were extrapolated both from the literature and from the Ascione survey instrument.

Subject offenses: Instant and all. Variables were provided to measure both the subject's instant and most serious offenses. The criminal histories of the subjects were screened to assure that any nonviolent offender with a violent prior offense would be disqualified from the study (see tables 4.2–4.5).

Cruelty to animals committed by subject. Variables were provided to measure cruelty to animals committed by the subject in each of the four categories (wild, farm, pet, and stray animals) designated by Ascione et al. (1997). Both Kellert and Felthous (1995) and Mead (1964) emphasized that cruelty committed toward *good* animals, such as *pets,* is of greatest significance to the relationship of cruelty to animals and later violence against humans.

Frequency and seriousness of cruelty committed by subject. Kellert and Felthous (1985) emphasized the importance of the frequency of cruel acts committed. Frequent acts of cruelty might represent a pattern of escalating violence that might ultimately include violence against humans. In the study by Kellert and Felthous, 25 percent of the aggressive criminals surveyed had reported committing five or more acts of cruelty to animals, compared to less than 6 percent of moderate and nonaggressive criminals (pp. 119–120). With respect to frequency, potential responses on the survey used for this study were *none, once, twice, three times, four times, five times, frequent nonspecific,* and *other.* Kellert and Felthous also emphasized the severity of the cruelty committed and provided a range of acts from which the *seriousness of* variable used in this study was constructed.

Subject response to cruelty committed by subject. Sensitivity toward animals and recognition of their sentience are critical factors in inhibiting and preventing cruelty to animals. Young children sometimes commit cruel acts because they perceive animals as objects devoid of feeling and the ability to experience distress and pain. Most children can be taught to appreciate animals and to express compassion for them. Some children will be motivated to commit cruel acts against animals, however, *because* of the animals' sentience. Such children take pleasure in the control that they can exhibit over animals and in the pain and fear that they have the power to inflict. Therefore, the subject's response to cruelty committed was viewed in this study as a critical factor with respect to the relationship. A subject's reported response to cruelty committed was coded to reflect *remorse, not cruel or no affect, emotional/psych release/thrill, sex satisfaction, power/control, sadism,* or *other.*

Cruelty to animals observed by subject. Studies such as DeViney, Dickert, and Lockwood (1983) and Ascione (1998) indicated that animal cruelty observed by children might be indicative of domestic violence. Furthermore, studies such as MacDonald (1961) conclude that parental brutality was a likely prognostic factor to future homicidal behavior. Therefore, on the assumption that familial violence might be a factor in both childhood cruelty to animals and later violence against humans, variables were included to measure cruelty committed by a family member and observed by the subject.

Variables were also included to measure observed cruelty committed by a friend or an acquaintance of the subject, also on the assumption that such cruelty might also influence childhood cruelty to animals, such as in the case of peer pressure. Finally, a variable was included to measure cruelty committed by a stranger and observed by the subject.

Frequency and seriousness of cruelty observed by subject. These variables are analogous to those previously described with respect to the frequency and seriousness of cruelty to animals committed by subject as extrapolated from the study by Kellert and Felthous (1985).

Subject response to cruelty observed. Likewise, these variables are analogous to the response variables with respect to cruelty committed by subject previously described. The exception is that a response of intervention was included to measure any instances in which the subject attempted to intervene on behalf of an abused animal. Potential responses to these variables were *intervention, remorse, not cruel or no affect, thrill, power/control, sadism,* and *other.*

Ascione variables: Frequency and severity of cruelty committed by subject. These variables were designed by Ascione et al. (1997) to quantify both the frequency and the severity of cruelty to animals committed by the subject. With respect to the *frequency* variable, the scoring process was as follows: A score of 0 indicated that no cruelty had been committed. A score of 1 indicated that one or two instances of cruelty had been committed. A score of 2 indicated that more than two, but fewer than six, instances of cruelty had been committed. A score of 3 indicated that more than six instances of cruelty had been committed.

With respect to the *severity* variable, the scoring process was as follows: A score of 0 indicated that either no cruelty had been committed or that no more than one instance of minor teasing behavior (behavior that did not cause pain or harm) toward an animal had been committed. A score of 1 indicated that repeated instances of such teasing behavior had been committed. A score of 2 indicated that one or more instances of acts of maltreatment had been committed that are presumed to have resulted in pain or discomfort to the animal (such as the loss of a feather, a minor eye irritation, a sprain or scratch, or a similar injury that would have elicited a distress vocalization from the animal). A score of 3 indicated one or more instances of maltreatment had been committed that are presumed to result in pain, such as acts that prolong suffering, torturing, and/or death.

Ascione variables: Covert and isolate. Ascione developed two variables to account for the influence of others to either facilitate or inhibit the subject's committing cruelty to animals. Ascione termed these variables *covert* and *isolate.* The category of *covert* was developed to reveal the effort or lack of effort that the subject displayed to conceal the cruel acts as they were performed. A score of 0 indicated that the subject had committed cruelty to animals in the presence of others who were participants. A score of 1 indicated that the subject had committed cruelty to animals in the presence of others who were not participants. A score of 2 indicated that the subject had committed cruelty to animals when the subject was alone. A score of 3 indicated that the subject had committed cruelty to animals secretly and had taken measures to conceal the cruelty.

The category of *isolate* addressed the issue of the persuasive influence of others, such as adult or peer pressure. A score of 0 indicated that no isolated acts of cruelty to animals had been committed by the subject. A score of 1 indicated that the subject was with one or more adults who were participants when the act of cruelty to animals was committed. A score of 2 indicated that the subject was with one or more peers when the act of cruelty was committed. A score of 3 indicated that the subject acted alone when the act of cruelty to animals was committed.

Ascione variables: Empathy. The category of empathy, analogous to the response variables used in this study, addressed the issue of the subject's sensitivity toward the animal that was the object of cruelty and the subject's recognition or failure to recognize the sentience of that animal. A score of 0 indicated that no cruelty had been committed. A score of 1 indicated that the subject expressed sensitivity with respect to the animal in question. A score of 2 indicated that the subject vacillated between expressing sensitivity and an uncaring, insensitive attitude. A score of 3 indicated that the subject displayed no sensitivity whatsoever but, instead, expressed delight in having caused the animal pain and distress.

Ascione variables: Sentience. The literature supporting the relationship between cruelty to animals and later violence against humans has often reported that cruelty against highly sentient animals is the most salient measure of this correlation. For example, Kellert and Felthous (1985) emphasized that cruelty to *pet* animals such as dogs and cats was particularly relevant to the relationship. Mead (1964) emphasized that cruelty toward good animals by the child might be a precursor to more violent acts committed later on. Ascione's variable with respect to sentience was, therefore, a crucial factor in this study.

Ascione differentiated between invertebrates such as worms and insects, cold-blooded vertebrates such as fish and reptiles, and warm-blooded vertebrates such as birds and mammals. Accordingly, these three types were included in this study.

Ascione variables: Diversity/cross and *diversity/within categories.* Ascione's *diversity/cross* variable compared cruelty committed by violent and nonviolent subjects with respect to animal category. It was designed to measure instances in which the subject had committed cruelty against more than one of the four animal types (wild, farm, pet, and stray). The scoring process for this variable was as follows: A score of 0 indicated that no cruelty had been committed. A score of 1 indicated that cruelty to animals had been committed against one of the four animal types. A score of 2 indicated that cruelty had been committed against two of the four animal types. A score of 3 indicated that cruelty had been committed against three or four of the four animal types.

Ascione's *diversity/within* variable compared nonviolent and violent subjects with respect to cruelty committed by the subject to animals within the same category, wild, farm, pet, or stray. The scoring process for this variable was as follows: A score of 0 indicated that no cruelty had been committed. A score of 1 indicated that cruelty had been committed against no more than two animals within a given category. A score of 2 indicated that cruelty had been committed against more than two, but fewer than six, animals within a given category. A score of 3 indicated that cruelty had been committed against more than six animals within a given category.

Past animal abuse resembling subject offenses. This variable was included to measure analogous acts committed by the subject against both animals and humans. The assumption was made that cruelty to animals and violence against humans involved a continuum of behavior. Accordingly, this variable was designed to measure acts against both animals and humans that were similar in kind. For example, if a subject had burned his victim to death and had reported previous cruelty including burning pet cats, this analogous behavior would be viewed as especially significant with respect to the relationship.

Heide variables: Abuse against subject. The literature has suggested that violent individuals are often the victims of parental abuse, or an otherwise violent familial environment, during childhood. The assumption is that violence is insidious and generates a cycle of victimization that crosses generations. A problem with this interpretation is that it has the potential not only to explain violence but also to excuse it. In identifying this problem, it is not the intent of this study to underestimate the power of victimization and its ability to scar its victims or to minimize the suffering of its victims. However, the fact remains that many victims of abuse become advocates against abuse rather than abusers.

The methodology used in this study applied rigorous attention to issues of definition and articulation with respect to the operative variables. Specific questions were asked to determine whether particular types of abuse occurred. For example, one question that addressed physical abuse was "Did a parent or guardian ever hit you because the parent or guardian was very angry?" Heide (1992) clearly defined four types of abuse: *verbal, sexual, physical,* and *psychological.*

Heide defined *physical abuse* as "inflicted physical injury or the attempt to inflict physical injury or pain that is indicative of the unresolved needs of the aggressor inappropriately expressed" (p. 19). For example, a reported beating by a subject that left bruises or broken bones was clearly physical abuse and was coded as such. A reported "occasional spanking," however, was not recorded as physical abuse.

Heide defined *verbal abuse* as "words spoken to a child, or remarks made in the child's presence about the child, that either are designed to damage the child's concept of self or would reasonably be expected to undermine a child's sense of competence and self-esteem" (p. 27). For example, reported verbal disputes between the subject and the subject's parents over the subject's choice of childhood friends or poor grades in school were not recorded as verbal abuse. If the disputes contained insults and otherwise demeaning remarks and criticisms, however, then they were recorded as verbal abuse.

With respect to *sexual abuse*, Heide distinguished between two types: *overt* and *covert*. Overt sexual abuse was defined as a physical form of offending, such as the behavior of a parent who sexually fondled a child or who engaged in vaginal intercourse, anal sex, or oral sex with a child. Heide defined covert abuse as the "exposing of a child to sexual issues that are age-inappropriate or as the raising of a child in a sexually saturated or provocative environment" (p. 22).

Heide noted that the terms "psychological abuse" and "verbal abuse" are sometimes used interchangeably by both professionals and the public. *Psychological abuse* "is a far broader term than verbal abuse, encompassing words and behaviors that undermine, or would reasonably be expected to undermine a child's sense of self, competence, and safety in the world" (p. 28). Physical and sexual abuse are also forms of psychological abuse when they are inflicted by a parent or guardian because "these acts represent a violation of trust" (p. 28).

The abuse variables used in this study were specific with respect to both type of abuse and the abuser. Variables were also provided to designate particular abusers within and outside the nuclear family, such as *biological mother, biological father, stepmother, stepfather, grandmother, uncle, religious figure, friend, neighbor,* etc. Variables were also provided to designate multiple abusers. Finally, to determine the pervasiveness of abuse, three additional variables were provided: *data consistent with abuse of any kind committed against the subject, abuse of at least two types,* and *abuse of at least three types.*

Heide variables: Familial dysfunction. Three variables were used in this study with respect to familial dysfunction. These variables were *documented familial dysfunction—subject's family of origin, data reported consistent with familial dysfunction—subject's family of origin,* and *suspected familial dysfunction—subject's family of origin.*

Unlike categories of abuse, precise definitions with respect to familial dysfunction are more difficult to formulate because perceptual views of familial dysfunction are often highly subjective. Therefore, the discernment of dysfunction as such by both the subject reporting it and the interviewer recording it is both a subjective process and a reciprocal one, because both parties carry their own perceptions and assumptions of familial normalcy into the interview process.

For example, the interviewer may have a midwestern, farming background including a nuclear family of parents married to each other and never divorced, as well as a similarly intact extended family of grandparents, uncles, aunts, and cousins. In addition, the farm might have been handed down through the generations, and there may be a strong sense of familial tradition. Therefore, a unique family culture has evolved on the basis of a history of coherence and stability. In the eyes of the interviewer, this type of family is normal. If the interviewer is also a Christian fundamentalist, then this perception of family would presumably be even more parochial.

Conversely, the subject may have reported a very different family orientation. For example, take a subject who reported that his parents are divorced and that he has no recollection of his natural father. Furthermore, the subject lived with his mother, who never remarried but had relationships with several boyfriends over the years. The subject described his mother as a "good" mother, even though she had very little time for the subject because there were several siblings, some by different fathers, and she had to work because her boyfriends seldom did. As a result "because money was often tight," the subject "lived on and off" with grandparents. The subject reported that his mother and her boyfriends often drank heavily, and sometimes there would be "arguments or an occasional fight" but "nothing serious." After an episode concerning a "particularly mean" boyfriend, however, the subject lived for a time with an aunt. In summary, although the subject reported that he was "independent" from an early age and that there was "no real supervision," he ultimately described his child-hood as "normal."

The familial scenario described by the subject poses a potential con-ceptual quagmire for the interviewer. In the interviewer's eyes, not only does the scenario reported by the subject appear to be dysfunctional, but, the subject is an offender, incarcerated for criminal behavior. The inter-viewer might assume, based on the subject's criminality, that familial dys-function was a factor operative in the subject's formative years.

Considering the above scenario, the question proposed is, Would the interviewer view the subject's family history and circumstances differently if the subject were presently a banker or a doctor rather than a prison in-mate? More specifically, does the success or failure of the subject in adult-hood *define* or *dispute* dysfunction?

Ultimately, it appears that dysfunction is obviously more than the sum of its parts. Accordingly, the interviewer must carefully consider the com-plex subjective factors operative in familial dysfunction. Objectivity and clarity of definition, however, can be, and indeed have been, applied to dysfunction. Heide (1992) articulated a typology of dysfunction that pro-vides operational and applicable precision. In dysfunctional families, "par-ents lack adequate parenting skills and are likely to abuse and neglect their offspring because issues from their own childhoods are unresolved and be-cause of their inadequate personal development" (p. 46).

Clearly, according to Heide's definition, the lack of parenting skills is often a key factor operative in the dynamics of familial dysfunction and can result in the child being abused and/or neglected. Abuse has already been defined and will be treated as conceptually independent from dys-function. Heide's definition of dysfunction, applied in concert with recog-nition on the part of the interviewer that subjectivity must yield to objectivity, will facilitate the application of a conceptually sound method-ology to address both the phenomenon and the processes of familial dys-function.

The subject previously described will serve as an example of this ap-plication. First, the interviewer should not assume that the subject expe-rienced familial dysfunction solely because the subject is a prison inmate. The deductive reasoning represented by that assumption fails to account for individuals who have experienced dysfunctional backgrounds and are not prison inmates. The subject's criminality must be taken into account, however, as part of a holistic and inductive assessment of the subject's familial background.

The subject reported that his childhood had very little structure and supervision. Clearly, most professionals and laypersons alike would agree that children require structure and adult supervision. The subject also described some of his mother's relationships with boyfriends as argumentative, including an "occasional fight," and reported that on one occasion he was compelled to live temporarily with an aunt owing to the behavior of a "particularly mean" boyfriend. Furthermore, the subject reported that both his mother and her boyfriends drank heavily and that the boyfriends "seldom worked." Clearly, the familial circumstances described by the subject, which included both verbal and physical altercations, alcohol abuse, and financial insecurity, would constitute dysfunction.

For purposes of this study, the scenario just described would be recorded as data reported consistent with familial dysfunction and as suspected familial dysfunction. However, documented familial dysfunction would not be recorded because the case file did not contain information about the subject's familial background. The conceptual methodology described above was consistently applied in this study.

Alcohol and drug abuse: Subject's family of origin. Variables were included to measure alcohol and/or drug abuse by parental figures within the subjects' family of origin.

Alcohol and drug use by subject. Variables were included to measure alcohol and drug use by the subject. Five categories of substance use were examined. These categories were *alcohol, marijuana, cocaine, heroin,* and *LSD.*

Psychological evaluation of subject. The subject's case history was examined for the presence of psychological evaluations, and variables were constructed to code relevant data. These results were *normal range, lack of self-esteem, magical thinking, anger management problems, lack of inhibition, subject in denial, sociopathic,* and *other.*

Age when subject first in trouble with the law. A variable was developed to compare age variations between nonviolent and violent subjects with respect to when they first got in trouble with the law. Potential responses were *over 30, age 22–30, age 18–21, age 13–17, age 9–12,* and *age 5–8.*

The next chapter describes the analyses undertaken to explore the link between animal cruelty and violence against humans. The findings include discussion of both quantitative and qualitative analyses.

Notes

1. Perusal of these lists confirmed that sample subjects were "randomly selected by computer"; that is, offenders were not in any numerical sequence (e.g., no. 165147 was followed by 544177, followed by 738102, followed by 118949, etc.) and the names of inmates were not listed in alphabetical order.

The computer lists for both violent and nonviolent offenders each contained the names of one hundred inmates. The institutional staff oversampled because they knew that (a) some inmates, when approached by the interviewer, would refuse to take part in the study; (b) other inmates would be unavailable for the interview process on any given date (e.g., in disciplinary confinement, ill); (c) others might have been moved to another facility when the interviewer was available to meet with them and, hence, would no longer be available at the site; and (d) some offenders who were identified as nonviolent based on the "primary offense" screening would be found by the interviewer when examining the case file or interviewing the offender to have committed violent prior offenses and would be omitted from further participation in the study. If on a given day when the interviewer arrived at the prison, an inmate on the list prepared for that day was unavailable (e.g., was in lockdown), another name was selected at random from the list. This occurred several times, especially among the violent group.

2. Chi-square is often utilized to evaluate the "goodness of fit" between an obtained set of frequencies in a random sample and what would be expected if no relationship existed between the variables under consideration. For example, there is no reason to expect that the violent and nonviolent offenders randomly selected for this study differed with respect to race, education, marital status, or number of children. Accordingly, the null hypothesis would state that no relationship exists between offender group (violent/nonviolent) and offender race, offender education, offender marital status, and offender children, each tested individually. Chi-square compares the frequencies obtained in each cell possibility with the cells expected if there is no relationship. This statistic allows us to determine if there is sufficient reason, based on the probability level chosen, to reject the null hypothesis of no differences between the violent and nonviolent offenders with respect to each of these demographic variables. (In analyses wherein one or more cells had fewer than five cases, Fisher's Exact Test, one tail, was used to determine statistical significance.) In this study, the probability level was set at less than .05, which means that the chances of erroneously rejecting the null hypothesis when it is true are less than five times out of one hundred.

CHAPTER FIVE
FINDINGS

The variables used in this study were designed for two purposes. The primary goal of the study was to evaluate whether acts of childhood cruelty toward four types of animals differentiated between violent and nonviolent adult offenders. Second, many of the variables were expressly designed to facilitate both quantitative and qualitative analyses. Variables were constructed to explore factors associated with cruelty to animals as well as numerous other phenomena that were suggested by the literature to bear relevance to the relationship of cruelty to animals and later violence against humans.

The null hypothesis would predict that no differences would be found between violent and nonviolent offenders with respect to animal cruelty. This hypothesis and its derivatives were tested using chi-square. We selected this statistic because it is an appropriate test of a relationship when dichotomous data are being used. Chi-square compares the frequencies obtained in each cell possibility with the cells expected if there was no relationship. This statistic allows us to determine if there is sufficient reason, based on the probability level chosen, to reject the null hypothesis of no differences between the violent and nonviolent offenders with respect to animal cruelty. In analyses wherein one or more cells had less than five cases, Fisher's Exact Test, one tail, was used to determine statistical significance. In this study, the probability level was set at less than .05, which means that the chances of erroneously rejecting the null hypothesis when it is true are less than five times out of one hundred.

Although the variables often had several values, many could be conceptualized as dichotomous. In light of the small sample size, these variables were frequently recoded when necessary and appropriate to permit quantitative analyses. Recoded variables were always identified as such.

Quantitative analyses with respect to specific animal category variables (wild, farm, pet, and stray animals) were often insufficient to substantiate statistical significance because the reported numbers were too small, given the overall sample size of ninety. Notwithstanding, the descriptive data extrapolated from these variables revealed compelling qualitative conclusions. Furthermore, the qualitative results of this study both stimulate and provide direction for further inquiry.

The analyses proceeded in six stages. The first set of analyses tested the hypothesis that addressed the essential issue as to whether or not there was a relationship between cruelty committed to animals and later acts of violence committed against humans. The second set of analyses tested the relationship of cruelty committed against each of the four animal types and later violence committed against humans. The third set of analyses tested the various Ascione variables, including *severity* and *frequency, covert* and *isolate, empathy, sentience,* and *diversity/cross* and *diversity/within* variables.

The fourth set of analyses tested the variables with respect to cruelty to animals observed by the subject. Some of the literature had suggested that observed violence might serve as a catalyst for later violence committed by the observer. The purpose of the variables with respect to cruelty to animals observed by the subject was to test the relationship of cruelty observed and later cruelty committed. The fifth set of analyses tested the subject responses to cruelty observed. It was expected that responses indicating expressed remorse and/or empathy would be tied to later acts of cruelty *not* committed.

The sixth set of analyses tested the relationship of the Heide variables with respect to cruelty to animals committed by subject. The Heide variables included *verbal, sexual, physical,* and *psychological abuse; family dysfunction; familial alcohol and drug abuse; alcohol and drug use by subject; psychological evaluation of the subject;* and *age when subject first in trouble with the law.* Much of the literature suggested that childhood exposure to familial violence and abuse served as a precursor to later acts of violence committed by the abused.

The Test of the Hypothesis: First Set of Analyses

The existant literature supporting a relationship between cruelty to animals and later violence against humans would suggest that this study would find a relationship when animal cruelty was examined within offender groups. Cruelty to animals is a complex phenomenon that requires complex inquiry. The study by Kellert and Felthous (1985), for example, examined the relationship by using a methodology based on precision of definition and conceptual clarity. The fact that their findings both substantiated a relationship and provided practical insights as to motives for cruelty strongly suggested the validity of the relationship. Furthermore, some of the studies that either did not support the relationship or that resulted in inconclusive findings (e.g., Climent, Hyg, & Erwin, 1972) used methodologies that were problematic or insufficient to appropriately address the issue.

The null hypothesis stated that there would be no statistically significant difference between the proportion of violent offenders who had committed past acts of cruelty to animals and the proportion of nonviolent offenders who had committed past acts of cruelty to animals. The null hypothesis was rejected.

As shown in table 5.1, chi-square analysis revealed that there was a statistically significant difference between the proportion of violent subjects (N = 45) who committed past acts of cruelty to animals and the proportion of nonviolent subjects (N = 45) who committed past acts of cruelty to animals (chi-square = 12.100; d.f. = 1; p = .00). The proportion of violent subjects who committed past acts of cruelty to animals was significantly greater (56 percent) than the proportion of nonviolent subjects (20 percent) who committed such acts.

A comparison of the Ascione summary scores comparing cruelty to animals committed by nonviolent and violent subjects with respect to severity, frequency, covert, isolate, and empathy also yielded statistically significant results. The summary scores variable was designed to provide a qualitative comparison of summary scores with respect to nonviolent and violent participants who had committed acts of cruelty against animals. (This variable was recoded to quantify the overall test of the hypothesis as discussed earlier.) The summary scores were determined by adding the scores for each of the five variables (by subject) within each group. The total scores for each group were then compared to each other (violent versus nonviolent). The summary scores revealed that a statistically significant greater proportion of violent subjects had scored higher (summary score 414) than the proportion of nonviolent subjects (summary score 101) (chi-square = 25.142; d.f. = 1; p = .033).

Table 5.1. Summary of Quantitative Analyses of Cruelty Committed by Subject by Animal Category (in percentages)

	Nonviolent			Violent				
Category	% Cruelty Committed	%No Cruelty Committed	N	% Cruelty Committed	% No Cruelty Committed	N	Chi-Square Results	Fisher's Exact Test
All Categories	20	80	45	56	44	45	12.100; d.f. = 1; p = .00*	p = .00*
Wild Animals	13	87	45	29	71	45	3.269; d.f. = 1; p = .07**	p = .06**
Farm Animals	2	98	45	13	87	45	.000; d.f. = 1; p = .05***	p = .05**
Pet Animals	7	93	45	24	76	45	6.133; d.f. = 1; p = .01*	p = .01*
Stray Animals	0	100	45	11	89	45	5.294; d.f. = 1; p = .02***	p = .03*

*Indicates significance.
**Levels .05–.07 are not statistically significant but indicate a tendency toward significance.
***Analyses nonapplicable: Cells < 5; Fisher's Exact Test, one tail, used to determine statistical significance.

Cruelty to Animals Committed by Subject: Second Set of Analyses

Quantitative analyses with respect to the four types of animals were compared for the two groups of offenders. As previously explained, Ascione's survey instrument explored cruelty to animals by dividing animals into four types: wild, farm, pet, and stray. Some of the literature had emphasized the significance of cruelty to pet animals with respect to the relationship of cruelty to animals and later violence against humans (Kellert & Felthous, 1995; Mead, 1964). Therefore, Ascione's survey was an important component of this study in that it facilitated both quantitative and qualitative analysis of the data with respect to specific animal types, including pet animals.

Quantitative analyses with respect to Ascione's summary score revealed statistical significance with respect to cruelty to animals when violent and nonviolent subjects were compared. Statistically significant differences were found between nonviolent and violent offenders in two of the four animal categories (pet and stray). In the remaining two categories (wild and farm), differences between the two offender groups just missed the level of significance. It seems likely that the results failed to reach significance owing to the small number of reports. The qualitative analyses with respect to farm and wild animals suggest that a relationship between cruelty to animals in these two categories and later violence against humans may indeed exist.

Pet Animals

As depicted in table 5.1 and consistent with theoretical predictions, statistical significance was demonstrated with respect to pet animals when violent and nonviolent subjects were compared (chi-square = 6.133; d.f. = 1; p = .013). The proportion of violent offenders (N = 45) who reported committing past acts of cruelty to pet animals was significantly greater (24 percent) than the proportion of nonviolent offenders (N = 45) who committed past acts of cruelty to pet animals (7 percent).

The data reported by three of the violent subjects were insufficient to establish that cruelty had been committed. Violent subjects also sometimes reported contradictory information. Cruelty committed was coded as such in this study only if the subject had positively articulated a committed act of animal cruelty. For example, one violent subject reported that his sister had purposely broken the neck of a kitten when he and his sister were children. The subject reported that the incident had taken place in the backyard of their home. At first the subject reported that his sister had been alone at the time of the incident because he had returned to the house. He later indicated that he and his sister had been together when the incident occurred. The contradictions with respect to the story suggested complicity. The subject stated, however, that he had not participated in the cruel act committed. Therefore, the incident was coded as *no cruelty committed* by subject.

The strength of the revealed relationship with respect to cruelty to pet animals when nonviolent and violent subjects were compared would have been stronger if dogfighting had not been found to be a confounding variable. The *seriousness of act committed* variables were included to qualitatively assess the specific types of acts of cruelty to animals committed. As shown in table 5.2, among nonviolent offenders, dogfighting

Table 5.2. Qualitative Summary of Most Serious Acts of Cruelty to Animals Committed by Subject (in real numbers)

	Wild		Farm		Pet		Stray	
Specific Act of Cruelty	N	V	N	V	N	V	N	V
Articulated Fear	1	0	0	0	0	0	0	0
Killed for Food	0	1	0	0	0	0	0	0
Killed for Sport	0	2	0	0	0	0	0	0
Tease/Torment/Deprive	0	0	0	1	0	1	0	0
Throw Object(s) At	0	0	0	1	0	0	0	0
Sex with Animal	0	0	0	1	0	2	0	0
Forced Fighting	0	0	0	0	3	1	0	0
Beating/Kicking/Stomping	0	1	0	2	0	1	0	1
Tying Animals Together	0	0	0	0	0	0	0	1
Shooting	5	7	1	1	0	1	0	0
Stabbing	0	1	0	0	0	0	0	0
Pouring Chemical Irritants On	0	0	0	0	0	2	0	0
Burning	0	0	0	0	0	0	0	1
Dismembering	0	1	0	0	0	0	0	1
Missing Data	0	0	0	0	0	3	0	1
Total Number	6	13	1	6	3	11	0	5

(*forced fighting*) was the most serious form of animal cruelty reported against pet animals. *In fact, in the case of nonviolent subjects, dogfighting was the only form of cruelty to pet animals reported.* In addition, two of the three nonviolent subjects who reported this act also reported that they shared their lives with *pet* dogs at the same time that they owned dogs for the express purpose of dogfighting. The subjects spoke of their pet dogs with fondness. One of the subjects described how his German shepherd, named Brownie, slept in his bed with him and lived to the age of ten, an age indicating that the dog received appropriate care during its lifetime.

Another factor indicating the confounding nature of dogfighting is the fact that all three of the nonviolent offenders who reported this act of cruelty were African American. All three subjects described dog-fights as a popular neighborhood activity that, despite its illegality, was attended by both adults and children. In most instances, gambling was the main attraction. In addition, the subjects claimed that the dogs involved were aggressive and wanted to fight. One offender reported that he considered it "cruel" to stop a fight because the methods that had to be used could injure a dog, "like poking a stick in the dog's ear to make him back down."

Considering the information that was reported by the nonviolent subjects, it appears that dogfighting, within the context of race (African American) and environment (urban), may be a confounding variable due to cultural factors. Interestingly, among the violent subjects, the only act of dogfighting committed was reported by a white subject who did not elaborate as to the particulars of motive or cultural context.

Although cruelty committed to pet animals was limited to dogfighting among the nonviolent subjects, acts of cruelty committed by violent subjects included a broad range of acts such as stomping a kitten to death, setting a dog on fire, and having sex with an animal. One violent subject reported having done something "very bad" to a puppy but "could not say" what it was. A similar report was made by another violent offender, who related that he had once "done something" to a pet animal but that he "could not talk about it."

As depicted in table 5.3, significant differences with respect to subject response to cruelty committed were not revealed as a result of the confounding factor of dogfighting. None of the three nonviolent subjects who reported participating in dogfighting viewed dogfighting as cruel but viewed it as a socially accepted activity within their cultural context. The responses provided by the nonviolent subjects with respect to the cruelty committed were also influenced by the confounding factor of dogfighting. Their responses to the cruelty committed included one response of *not cruel or no affect* and two responses of *emotional/psych release/thrill*. As will be discussed further, qualitative data also revealed that the subjects' conceptualizations of dogfighting were a crucial factor in understanding their attitudes toward the animals and the act of dogfighting. Finally, responses of *power/control* and *sadism* were reported only by violent subjects.

Wild Animals

Significance was not demonstrated when nonviolent and violent subjects were compared with respect to wild animals (chi-square = 3.269; d.f. = 1; p = .070). Both violent and nonviolent subjects described acts of cruelty to wild animals in various contexts. As depicted in table 5.1, although statistical significance was not established, a tendency toward significance was suggested in the predicted direction. More violent subjects (29 percent; N = 45) than nonviolent subjects (13 percent; N = 45) had committed cruelty to wild animals.

As depicted in table 5.2, twelve of the nineteen types of acts of cruelty committed against wild animals by the subjects involved shooting an animal. Some of the subjects reported these acts within the context of acts that conformed to acceptable levels of behavior within certain cultural parameters, such as shooting wild birds as a prelude to legitimate hunting or playing "war games." Four of the six nonviolent subjects who reported cruelty committed to a wild animal described their committed acts within this context. These four subjects described their acts of cruelty to wild animals as follows. One subject reported that at the age of nine, he shot a bird while "playing army" and felt remorse. A second subject reported that, while an adolescent, he had hunted rabbits, birds, and wild ducks with his brother. The subject described these acts as something he "grew out of." A third subject reported that, when he was thirteen or fourteen years old, he had hunted rabbits for "target practice." The subject described these acts as "ridiculous if you don't need food." A fourth subject reported that he learned how to hunt with a BB gun as a young child and that he later hunted rabbits, quail, and raccoons "mostly for food," using rifles and shotguns. The subject further reported that he had since lost all interest in hunting and that he "could no longer buy meat because there's not many animals left."

Many of the subjects reported that they had committed such acts with peers. *However, only violent offenders reported cruelty committed to a wild animal when alone.* For example, one violent subject reported that he "would go off on his own to shoot squirrels for the fun of it." Another violent subject reported that when he was in the sixth grade he would "go into the woods alone to shoot birds and other animals just to kill them." In contrast, one nonviolent offender reported that when he was nine years old he shot a bird with a BB gun while "playing war games with friends." He also reported that he "felt so bad" he broke his gun.

Among the two remaining nonviolent subjects who reported cruelty committed against wild animals, one of the subjects reported that, when he was eight to ten years old, he had shot raccoons with a BB gun "just as something to do" because he was a "spoiled brat" and cared little for the feelings of others. The subject further reported that as an adult he remained "self-centered," an attribute he blamed on his "permissive upbringing." The second subject reported that as an adolescent he "beat up a big snake out of fear," even though the snake had attempted to escape. The subject reported that he had "held up the dead snake for neighborhood kids to see," presumably to demonstrate that he was brave and had overcome his fear. The subject reported no other acts of cruelty to animals.

Of the thirteen violent subjects who reported cruelty committed to a wild animal, only two characterized the acts as a prelude to legitimate hunting. Most often the subjects reported that they committed acts either as "just something to do" or as acts committed "just to kill." For example, one violent subject reported that he and his friends had killed "whatever" wild animals they could find with "rocks, BB guns, slingshots, and rocket launchers." The subject also reported that often the animals were not killed but "merely wounded and left to die." He further reported that to the present day he "had no regrets." Violent subjects also reported such acts of cruelty as stabbing and dismembering. One subject reported that, as a child, he had enjoyed dismembering live fish he had caught while fishing.

Distinct qualitative differences between the subjects' responses were apparent when nonviolent and violent subject responses were compared.

As shown in table 5.3, a response of *remorse* was reported by two of the six nonviolent subjects but by only one of the eleven violent offenders who had reported cruelty committed to wild animals. Most of the nonviolent subjects described these childhood acts of cruelty as "foolish" or "childish" or as behavior that they "grew out of." Whereas most of the nonviolent offenders suggested that these acts had been inappropriate, most of the violent subjects either did not pass judgment as to their acts or reported that the cruelty they committed was "fun." Ten of the thirteen violent subjects reported a response of *not cruel or no affect* or *emotional/psych release/thrill.* The only sadistic act committed against a wild animal was reported by a violent offender.

Farm Animals

As table 5.1 shows, the number of incidents of cruelty to farm animals was insufficient to test statistical significance when violent and nonviolent subjects were compared using chi-square, so Fisher's Exact Test, one tail, was used ($p = .05$). Only one of the nonviolent subjects (2 percent) had reported cruelty committed to a farm animal compared to six (13 percent) of the violent offenders. The context in which the reported acts of cruelty occurred provided significant qualitative comparisons when nonviolent and violent subjects were compared. Comparisons with respect to the subjects' responses to cruelty committed also revealed compelling qualitative differences.

Table 5.3. Qualitative Summary of Subject Responses to Cruelty to Animals Committed by Subject (in real numbers)

	Animal Category							
	Wild		Farm		Pet		Stray	
	Subject Type							
Subject Response	N	V	N	V	N	V	N	V
Remorse	2	1	1	0	0	1	0	0
Not Cruel or No Affect	3	5	0	4	1	7	0	1
Emotional/Psych Release/Thrill	1	5	0	1	2	1	0	2
Power or Control	0	0	0	0	0	1	0	1
Sadism	0	1	0	0	0	1	0	1
Missing Data	0	1	0	1	0	0	0	0
Total Number	6	13	1	6	3	11	0	5

N = Nonviolent offender
V = Violent offender

As depicted in table 5.2, the only act of cruelty to a farm animal reported by a nonviolent subject involved shooting an animal. The subject described shooting a pig when he was eight years old. The subject's grandfather had given him his first "real gun," a rifle, as a birthday gift. Prior to this occasion, the subject had only used a BB gun, and he reported that he wanted to "test what the gun could do." To this end, he shot and killed a neighbor's pig. The subject reported that he had not given any thought to the pig's being a sentient creature. Rather, he had viewed the animal merely as an object to test his new rifle. His grandfather, however, viewed the act differently. He broke the subject's gun and ordered him to assist with chores on the neighbor's farm for a year. The subject reported that he felt remorse for his act. This particular act of reported cruelty is highly significant in light of Mead's (1964) warning that a lack of punishment for an act of cruelty committed to an animal by a child is worse than punishment that is too harsh.

As depicted in table 5.2, the most serious acts reported by the six violent subjects who reported cruelty committed to a farm animal were varied. (To reiterate, the variables with respect to the *seriousness of act committed* were designed to indicate the most serious act of cruelty committed by a given offender. Therefore, a given offender may have reported more than one act of cruelty committed within any of the four animal categories.) One of the six violent subjects who had reported cruelty committed to farm animals reported that he had teased animals. Another reported that he had thrown rocks at a cow "to hurt it." One of these subjects reported having had sex with a farm animal. Two subjects reported acts that involved the beating of an animal. One of these two subjects, for example, reported that, when he was eight years old, he had beaten a baby chick to death with a Coke bottle. The sixth reported that he had shot an animal to death.

As depicted in table 5.3, none of the violent subjects reported a response of *remorse*. For example, despite the brutality of the act involving the baby chick (which was rendered unidentifiable), the subject reported only that he was "not an animal person" and that he "liked to throw stuff." This subject's response was coded as *not cruel or no affect*. Three of the remaining violent subjects who had reported cruelty committed to farm animals also reported a response of *not cruel or no affect*. One of the six subjects did not provide a response, and this was coded as *missing data;* one subject reported a *thrill* response.

Stray Animals

As depicted in table 5.1, no acts of cruelty to stray animals were reported by nonviolent subjects. Cruelty was reported by five (11 percent) of the violent subjects. Fisher's Exact Test, one tail, and a better test to use, indicated that these differences were statistically significant.

As shown in table 5.2, the acts of cruelty reported by the five violent subjects included beating an animal, tying animals together (in order to watch them panic and fight to separate themselves), setting an animal on fire or otherwise burning an animal, and dismembering an animal. One of the violent subjects reported that he had committed many acts of violence toward animals but did not wish to be specific; his response was coded as *missing data.*

Although none of the nonviolent subjects reported cruelty committed to a stray animal, one nonviolent subject reported an act of self-defense involving a stray animal. The subject described being attacked by a stray dog while riding his bicycle and hitting the dog with a stick to make him "back off." Despite the circumstances of the incident, the subject reported that hitting the dog made him "feel sad."

Among those violent offenders who reported cruelty committed to a stray animal, none reported a response of *remorse.* Rather, as depicted in table 5.3, the responses reported by the violent subjects included *not cruel or no affect, thrill, power or control,* and *sadism.*

The one violent subject who reported a response of *power or control* described how, when he was an adolescent, he would "frequently" go into the woods with his hunting dogs "to stalk and overpower" his prey. The subject reported that he spear-hunted both wild animals and stray dogs "for the joy of the kill." The fact that the subject articulated that "control" was the primary motivation of the acts of cruelty committed distinguishes the *power and control* response from the *thrill* response in this case. A police report of the subject's crimes described how the subject "killed his victims in the woods and then dragged the bodies deeper into the woods." The subject's psychological evaluation noted that he reported that "many of my dreams are about the woods." The evaluation concluded that the subject had a sociopathic personality. In addition to first-degree murder, the subject's crimes included kidnapping and rape.

Past Animal Abuse Resembling Subject Offenses

Past acts of cruelty to animals resembling either the subject's instant or most serious offense, as suggested by the case referenced above, were reported only by violent offenders. One violent subject, a repeat sex offender, had been convicted while an adolescent of a *crime against nature* for sodomizing a reformatory pig. Another subject, convicted of *sexual battery on a person sixty-five years or older,* described how he would throw stones and bricks at stray animals "to beat and hurt them like my parents hurt me." According to the police report, the victim's face had been severely beaten.

Another violent subject had been previously arrested for *illegal hunting* and *poaching.* He was convicted of murdering his wife. The victim had been eviscerated with a buck knife. This example is provided for informational purposes only, because the subject did not complete the interview process and was not included in the study.

Ascione Variables: Third Set of Analyses

The Ascione variables were designed to analyze data among the four animal types (wild, pet, farm, and stray). As a result, the reported numbers with respect to these variables often remained insufficient to permit quantitative analyses. Whenever possible, the variables were recoded in order to permit statistical analysis. However, qualitative comparisons, rather than quantitative, were provided with respect to most of the Ascione variables. The results of the quantitative analyses with respect to the Ascione variables are depicted in table 5.4.

Severity and Frequency

Recoded variables permitted quantitative analyses of the *severity* and *frequency* variables with respect to the wild and pet animal categories. The severity variable was dichotomized to compare two values of behavior toward animals. The first value included either no acts of cruelty committed or minor acts committed that would not have caused physical harm to the animals; the second measure included all other acts of cruelty committed. The frequency variables were also recoded to compare two values. The

Table 5.4. Summary of Quantitative Analyses of Recoded Ascione Variables (in percentages)

Variable	Nonviolent		Violent		Chi-Square Results
	%	N	%	N	
Severity: Wild (Most severe)	13	45	29	45	**3.269; d.f. = 1; p = .070
Frequency: Wild (2 + acts)	9	45	24	45	*3.920; d.f. = 1; p = .048
Empathy: Wild (Vacillating or none)	7	45	27	45	*6.480; d.f. = 1; p = .010
Severity: Pet (Most severe)	7	45	22	45	*4.405; d.f. = 1; p = .035
Frequency: Pet (2 + acts)	7	45	9	45	.155; d.f. = 1; p = .694
Empathy: Pet (Vacillating or none)	7	45	22	45	*4.406; d.f. = 1; p = .036
Diversity/Cross (2–4 animal types)	2	45	20	45	*11.467; d.f. = 2; p = .003
Diversity/Within (3 + animals)	13	45	29	45	*9.727; d.f. = 2; p = .008

*Indicates significance.
**Not significant but demonstrates a tendency toward significance.

first value included either no acts of cruelty committed or no more than one act of cruelty committed; the second measure included two or more acts of cruelty committed.

As shown in table 5.4, the findings just missed the level of statistical significance in the category of wild animals with respect to *severity* (chi-square = 3.269; d.f. = 1; p = .070) when nonviolent and violent subjects were compared. The findings, however, were in the expected direction. The proportion of violent subjects who had committed acts of greatest severity (29 percent) was greater than the proportion of nonviolent subjects (13 percent). The results were statistically significant with respect to *frequency* (chi-square = 3.920; d.f. = 1; p = .048) in the category of wild animals when nonviolent subjects (N = 45) and violent subjects (N = 45) were compared. A significantly greater proportion of violent subjects committed acts of highest frequency (24 percent) when compared to the proportion of nonviolent subjects (9 percent). To review, most of the subjects, both nonviolent and violent, who had reported acts of cruelty committed to wild animals, had done so within the context of shooting them. In most cases, the animals involved were either killed outright or mortally wounded. Therefore, the cruelty committed by both nonviolent and violent subjects was severe in most cases. However, violent offenders reported more frequent participation than nonviolent subjects.

With respect to pet animals, statistical significance was demonstrated with respect to *severity* (chi-square = 4.405; d.f. = 1; p = .035). A significantly greater proportion of violent subjects had committed acts of greatest severity (22 percent) than had nonviolent subjects (7 percent). Statistical significance was not revealed with respect to *frequency* of cruelty to pet animals (chi-square = .155; d.f. = 1; p = .694; Fisher's Exact Test, one tail = .5) when nonviolent (N = 45) and violent subjects (N = 45) were compared. The proportion of violent subjects who had committed acts of highest frequency (9 percent) was analogous to the proportion of nonviolent subjects (7 percent). These findings were expected because of the significance already demonstrated with respect to pet animals (chi-square = 6.133; d.f. = 1; p = .01) and because of the consequences of the confounding factor of dogfighting previously addressed. To review, the only type of cruelty committed to pet animals reported by nonviolent subjects had been *forced fighting* (dogfighting). The nonviolent subjects who had reported participation in dogfighting had also reported frequent participation. However, although dogfighting is a severe form of animal cruelty, a significantly greater number of violent subjects had reported severe acts of cruelty committed to pet animals. These acts included stomping a kitten to death and throwing a puppy out of a fourth-story window.

Despite recoding, the reported numbers in the categories of farm and stray animals remained insufficient to permit quantitative analyses. No acts of cruelty to stray animals were reported by nonviolent subjects, and only one nonviolent subject reported cruelty to a farm animal. However, the violent subjects who had reported cruelty committed to stray animals had also reported frequent acts of cruelty committed.

Covert and Isolate

After recoding, the reported numbers in the categories of covert and isolate remained insufficient to do quantitative analyses. However, some qualitative distinctions are worthy of note. To review, only one nonviolent offender reported cruelty committed to a farm animal. Furthermore, no acts of cruelty committed to stray animals were reported by nonviolent subjects.

Most of the subjects, both violent and nonviolent, who reported cruelty committed to wild animals also reported that they had committed the acts either alone or with peers. The two *covert* acts (acts involving intentional concealment) of cruelty reported, however, were both reported by violent subjects.

With respect to pet animals, four of the eleven violent subjects who reported cruelty reported that their acts had been covert, and eight of these eleven reported that they had committed cruelty when alone, or *isolate*. Conversely, the acts of dogfighting reported by nonviolent subjects, which was the only type of cruelty reported by nonviolent offenders, involved a very public form of cruelty, despite its illegality.

Empathy

The Ascione category of *empathy*, analogous to the response variables already discussed, is especially important in view of the relationship of cruelty to animals and later violence against humans. The empathy variable was recoded into two values to facilitate quantitative analyses of two measurements. The first included either no cruelty committed or cruelty committed that was accompanied by clearly expressed remorse. The second value included cruelty committed for which the subject vacillated between feelings of remorse and uncaring and cases in which the subject expressed delight with respect to the cruelty committed.

Although the numbers reported for farm and stray animals remained insufficient to permit quantitative analyses, it is important to note that none of the eleven violent subjects who reported cruelty committed to animals within these categories expressed empathy. Conversely, the one nonviolent offender who reported cruelty to a farm animal clearly expressed empathy. To reiterate, no acts of cruelty committed to stray animals were reported by nonviolent subjects.

As depicted in table 5.4, statistical significance was revealed with respect to empathy in the categories of wild animals (chi-square = 6.480; d.f. = 1; p = .010) and pet animals (chi-square = 4.406; d.f. = 1; p = .036) when nonviolent subjects (N = 45) and violent subjects (N = 45) were compared. With respect to wild animals, the proportion of nonviolent subjects who had either committed no acts of cruelty or who expressed empathy was significantly larger (93 percent) than the proportion of violent offenders (73 percent). Furthermore, the proportion of violent subjects who did not express empathy was significantly greater (27 percent) than the proportion of nonviolent subjects (7 percent) who did not express empathy.

With respect to pet animals, the proportion of nonviolent subjects who had either committed no acts of cruelty to pet animals or who expressed empathy was significantly larger (93 percent) than the proportion of violent offenders (78 percent). Stated conversely, the proportion of violent subjects who did not express empathy (22 percent) was significantly greater than the proportion of nonviolent subjects (7 percent). It must be reiterated, however, that with respect to pet animals, dogfighting was determined to be a confounding factor. Although none of the three nonviolent subjects who reported participation in dogfighting expressed remorse or empathy, they offered explanations for their attitudes with respect to dogfighting and the animals involved. Interestingly, they reported that it would have been crueler had they *not* allowed the dogs to fight because "they were meant to fight." In essence, by viewing dogfighting from the viewpoint of a seeming *perceptual inversion,* the subjects appeared to believe that they were indeed empathizing with their fighting dogs by allowing them to fight.

Sentience

The reported numbers with respect to two of the three categories of sentience were insufficient to permit quantitative analysis. With one exception, all of the acts of animal cruelty reported by the subjects involved warm-blooded vertebrates. Although not statistically significant, the proportion of violent subjects who had committed cruelty to warm-blooded vertebrates was greater (53 percent) than the proportion of nonviolent subjects who had committed cruelty to warm-blooded vertebrates (18 percent). The one reported act of cruelty to a cold-blooded vertebrate was reported by a nonviolent subject (2 percent). Neither violent nor nonviolent subjects reported cruelty committed to invertebrate animals.

Diversity/Cross and Diversity/Within

To reiterate, the study by Kellert and Felthous (1985) had concluded that the *frequency* of cruelty committed to animals was an important factor with respect to the relationship of cruelty to animals and later violence against humans. The Ascione variables *diversity/cross* and *diversity/within* were designed to measure the frequency of committed acts of cruelty both across and within the four animal types (wild, farm, pet, and stray).

These variables were recoded to permit quantitative analyses. The diversity/cross variable was recoded in order to compare three values: no cruelty committed, cruelty committed against no more than one of the four types of animals, and cruelty committed against two to four of the animal types.

As depicted in table 5.4, statistical significance was revealed with respect to Ascione's recoded *diversity/cross* variable (chi-square = 11.467; d.f. = 2; p = .003) when nonviolent and violent subjects were compared. The proportion of violent subjects who had committed cruelty against two to four types of animals was significantly greater (20 percent) than the proportion of nonviolent subjects who had committed cruelty against two to four types of animals (2 percent). The proportion of violent subjects who had committed cruelty to animals with respect to one of the four animal categories (29 percent) was significantly greater than the proportion of nonviolent subjects who had committed cruelty to animals with respect to one of the four animal categories (16 percent).

Ascione's *diversity/within* variable was recoded to compare three values: no acts of cruelty committed with respect to animals within one of the four animal categories, no more that two acts of cruelty committed, and three or more acts of cruelty committed. Statistical significance was also revealed with respect to Ascione's *diversity/within* variable (chi-square = 9.727; d.f. = 2; p = .008) when nonviolent (N = 45) and violent subjects (N = 45) were compared. The proportion of violent subjects who had committed cruelty to three or more animals within a given animal category was significantly greater (29 percent) than the proportion of nonviolent subjects who had committed cruelty to three or more animals within a given category (13 percent). Furthermore, the proportion of violent subjects who had committed cruelty to more than two animals within a given category was significantly greater (22 percent) than the proportion of nonviolent subjects who had committed cruelty to no more than two animals within a given category (7 percent).

Cruelty to Animals Observed by Subject: Fourth Set of Analyses

The *cruelty to animals observed by subject* variables were included as a means to explore the possible connection between exposure to violence and violence committed. Some of the literature discussed earlier (e.g., Owens & Straus, 1975; Sendi & Blomgren, 1975) had suggested that exposure to violence can generate what has come to be termed the *cycle of violence* whereby those individuals who have been exposed to violence go on to commit acts of violence against others. The variables with respect to *cruelty committed by other observed by subject* were designed to examine both quantitative and qualitative data with respect to specific acts of animal cruelty committed by others, which had been observed by the subjects. The four categories of animal abusers were family members, friends, acquaintances, and strangers.

On the basis of the literature, it was anticipated that more violent than nonviolent subjects would have been exposed to cruelty to animals. The results, however, indicated otherwise. Both nonviolent and violent subjects had been exposed to a wide range of violence committed by a variety of animal abusers. Overall, nonviolent subjects reported sixty-seven observed acts of cruelty to animals and violent subjects reported seventy-five acts of observed cruelty. Numerous analogous comparisons were revealed with respect to the number of acts of cruelty observed, the category of abuser, and the animal type abused when violent and nonviolent subjects were compared. For example, with respect to observed cruelty committed against pet animals by a friend, nonviolent subjects reported seven observed acts of cruelty and violent subjects reported eight acts. Similarly, in the category of observed cruelty committed against stray animals by an acquaintance, nonviolent subjects reported thirteen observed acts of cruelty and violent subjects reported twelve.

The qualitative findings also revealed that similar types of cruelty had been observed by nonviolent and violent subjects. For example, with respect to the abuser category of family member, both nonviolent and violent subjects reported observed acts of cruelty that included the beating of an animal, the prolonged slaughter of an animal, the choking or suffocating of an animal, the feeding of a dangerous substance (such as broken glass) to an animal, and the teasing and/or tormenting of an animal.

One qualitative difference, however, with respect to cruelty observed by subject when nonviolent and violent subjects were compared is worthy of note. Despite the apparently similar levels of exposure of nonviolent and violent subjects to acts of cruelty committed by others, several of the violent subjects who reported observed cruelty also reported that they had observed the same friend commit cruelty on more than one occasion. For example, one violent offender reported that he had, on two separate occasions, observed the same friend stone to death a "baby pig" and a dog. Although the subject did not report any involvement in these acts of cruelty, and thus none was recorded, the repetitive nature of the cruelty observed by the subject suggests complicity. Furthermore, the question must be raised as to why the subject continued to associate with such a friend if the subject was opposed to the cruelty committed.

On the basis of the literature supporting the connection of violence observed and violence committed, further study with respect to these variables is required. *Empathy* is a critical factor operative with respect to violence observed and later violence committed. As indicated by the Ascione empathy variables previously discussed, a significant perceptual distinction between nonviolent and violent subjects has been the expression of empathy toward abused animals. The following analyses with respect to *subject response to cruelty committed by others* reinforce the validity of this finding.

Subject Response to Cruelty Committed by Others: Fifth Set of Analyses

The *subject response to cruelty committed by other* variables were designed to operate in tandem with the Ascione *empathy* variables. The purpose of the Ascione *empathy* variables was to quantify empathy. The purpose of the response variables was to qualitatively compare nonviolent and violent subjects with respect to their feelings and/or attitudes toward the cruelty that they had observed.

Potential responses were *intervention, remorse, not cruel or no affect, thrill, power/control*, and *sadism*. A subject response of *intervention* or *remorse* indicated that the subject had empathized with the animal being abused. A response of *not cruel or no affect* indicated that the subject either had ambivalent feelings toward the animal or that the subject did not view the act as cruel, as shooting wild birds for "target practice" or dogfighting, which was viewed as more of a "sport" than a form of animal cruelty. Responses of *thrill, power/control,* and *sadism,* however, indicated that the subject recognized that the observed acts were cruel but that he nonetheless achieved satisfaction or enjoyment from them. The qualitative findings with respect to these variables are depicted in table 5.5.

Pet Animals

Seventeen cases of observed cruelty to pet animals were reported by nonviolent subjects, and twenty cases were reported by violent subjects. Although the number of reports by the two groups was similar, the qualitative differences between the responses were pronounced.

A response of *intervention* was reported five times by nonviolent offenders, whereas none of the violent offenders reported this response. Responses of *power/control* and *sadism* were reported only by violent offenders. To illustrate the range of responses, one violent subject reported that he had observed an acquaintance bury a cat, leaving its head exposed, and then decapitate the animal with a lawnmower. The subject described the acquaintance as "crazy" but expressed no remorse about the incident. Conversely, a nonviolent subject reported that his friend had owned a dog that he kept chained in the backyard, an act

Table 5.5. **Qualitative Summary of Subject Responses to Cruelty to Animals Committed by Other (in real numbers)**

	Animal Category							
	Wild		Farm		Pet		Stray	
	Subject Type							
Subject Response	N	V	N	V	N	V	N	V
Intervention	0	0	0	0	5	0	3	2
Remorse	5	2	7	3	6	4	10	1
Not Cruel or No Affect	0	4	1	7	3	11	3	16
Thrill	2	2	0	0	3	1	1	1
Power or Control	0	0	0	0	0	1	0	0
Sadism	0	1	0	0	0	2	0	0
Other	0	0	0	0	0	1	0	0
Total Number	7	9	8	10	17	20	17	20

N = Nonviolent
V = Violent

that the subject considered cruel. It was explained to the subject that the act described constituted neglect, perhaps, but not cruelty and would not be recorded as cruelty observed. The subject responded that, despite any legal interpretations, he still considered the act to be an act of cruelty to animals.

Wild Animals

To reiterate, most of the nonviolent subjects who had committed cruelty to wild animals had done so within the context of the cruelty being a prelude to legitimate hunting or playing "war games," often in the company of others. Most of the nonviolent subjects who reported observed cruelty to wild animals did so within an analogous context. For example, these subjects most frequently reported observed cruelty to wild animals that was committed by friends, by an older sibling, or by a relative.

Qualitative differences were revealed when the responses of nonviolent and violent subjects were compared. Five of the seven nonviolent subjects who reported cruelty observed committed against a wild animal reported a response of *remorse*. Two of the nonviolent subjects reported a response of "fun," which was coded as a *thrill* response. A response of *remorse*, however, was reported by only two of the nine violent subjects who had reported observed acts of cruelty committed by others against a wild animal. Four of the nine subjects reported a response of *not cruel or no affect*, two reported a response of *thrill*, and one reported a response of *sadism*.

Farm Animals

In the category of farm animals, qualitative differences were especially revealed when nonviolent subjects were compared to violent subjects with respect to the responses of *remorse* and *not cruel or no affect*. Seven of the eight nonviolent subjects who reported observed acts of cruelty committed by others against farm animals reported a response of *remorse*. Only one of the nonviolent subjects reported a response of *not cruel or no affect*. Conversely, seven of the ten violent subjects who had reported observed acts of cruelty reported a response of *not cruel or no affect*. Only three of the violent subjects reported a response of *remorse*.

Stray Animals

With respect to stray animals, marked differences were revealed when the subject responses of *remorse* and *not cruel or no affect* were compared between the two groups of subjects. Whereas ten of the seventeen nonviolent subjects who observed cruelty committed by others reported a response of *remorse*, such a response was reported by only one of the twenty violent subjects who observed cruelty committed by others. Furthermore, a response of *not cruel or no affect* was reported by sixteen of the violent subjects and three of the nonviolent subjects.

Heide Variables: Sixth Set of Analyses

Abuse against Subject

The abuse variables were designed to reveal both quantitative and qualitative data with respect to childhood abuse reported by the subjects. The two variables addressing abuse of *at least two types* and abuse *of at least three types* were designed to provide quantitative comparisons with respect to the two groups of subjects. As depicted in table 5.6, the variable with respect to abuse of *any kind* and the four variables addressing the specific types of abuse (*verbal, sexual, physical,* and *psychological*) were designed to reveal qualitative and comparative insights as to the identity of the abusers (e.g., biological mother, biological father, stepmother).

Table 5.6. Qualitative Summary of Abuse against Subject (in percentages)

	Type of Abuse									
	% Any Kind		% Verbal		% Sexual		% Physical		% Psychological	
Abuser Type	N	V	N	V	N	V	N	V	N	V
No Abuse	30	28	36	14	88	91	30	24	0	0
Biological Mother	9	7	3	7	0	0	6	7	13	10
Biological Father	11	9	6	14	0	4	10	14	16	13
Stepmother	2	0	3	0	0	0	3	0	3	0
Stepfather	2	5	3	7	8	0	3	7	3	7
More than One Above	34	35	39	44	4	4	33	38	48	53
Other	11	16	10	14	0	0	13	10	16	17
N	44	43	31	29	26	22	30	29	31	30

Note: No statistical significance was demonstrated when nonviolent and violent subjects were compared.

N = Nonviolent
V = Violent

On the basis of the conclusions of some of the literature cited, it was expected that a significantly greater proportion of violent than nonviolent subjects would have reported exposure to abuse. The results, however, indicated that both nonviolent and violent subjects had been exposed to significant levels of abuse. Physical and verbal abuse were pervasive within both groups of offenders. Of subjects who reported abuse, 64 percent of the nonviolent subjects reported *verbal* abuse compared to 86 percent of the violent subjects, and 70 percent of the nonviolent subjects reported *physical* abuse compared to 76 percent of the violent subjects. All of the subjects who reported abuse also reported exposure to *psychological* abuse.

The Heide variables were recoded to permit quantitative analyses of the variables. The results of these analyses are depicted in table 5.7. The abuse of *any kind* variable was recoded to quantitatively compare two values—no abuse of any kind reported and abuse of any of the four types reported—with respect to the two groups of subjects. Statistical significance

Table 5.7. Summary of Quantitative Analyses of Recoded Heide Abuse Variables (in percentages)

Category	Nonviolent	N	Violent	N	Chi-Square Results
Abuse Any Kind					
No	30		28		
Yes	70	44	72	43	.029; d.f. = 1, p = .866
Abuse 2 Types					
(0–1 Type)	47		36		
(at least 2 Types)	53	45	64	45	1.15; d.f. = 1; p = .284
Abuse 3 Types					
(0–2 Types)	58		56		
(at least 3 Types)	42	45	44	45	.045; d.f. = 1; p = .832
Verbal Abuse					
No abuse/verbal	56		44		
Yes verbal	44	45	56	45	1.111; d.f. = 1; p = .292
Sexual Abuse					
No abuse/sexual	93		96		
Yes sexual	7	45	4	45	.212; d.f. = 1; p = .645[+]
Physical Abuse					
No abuse/physical	53		51		
Yes physical	47	45	49	45	.045; d.f. = 1; p = .833
Psychological Abuse					
No abuse/psych	31		33		
Yes psych	69	45	67	45	.051; d.f. = 1; p = .821

Note: No statistical significance revealed.

[+]Fisher's Exact Test = .5

was not revealed with respect to this variable (chi-square = .029; d.f. = 1; p = .866) when nonviolent (N = 44) and violent (N = 43) subjects were compared. The proportion of nonviolent subjects who reported abuse of any kind was 70 percent compared to 72 percent of violent offenders.

Significance was also not revealed with respect to the abuse *of at least two types* (chi-square = 1.147; d.f. = 1; p = .284) and abuse *of at least three types* (chi-square = .045; d.f. = 1; p = .831) variables when nonviolent (N = 45) and violent subjects (N = 45) were compared. The variable with respect to *at least two types* of abuse was recoded to include two values: no abuse reported or abuse of no more than one type reported, and at least two types of abuse reported. The variable with respect to *at least three types* of abuse was recoded to include no abuse reported or no more than two types of abuse reported, and at least three types of abuse reported. Fifty-three percent of the nonviolent subjects reported at least two types of abuse compared to 64 percent of the violent subjects. Forty-two percent of the nonviolent subjects had reported abuse of at least three types compared to 44 percent of the violent subjects.

The Heide variables with respect to the four specific types of abuse were recoded to quantitatively compare two values: no abuse of any kind or no abuse of the kind specified by the variable, and abuse of the kind specified by the variable (i.e., verbal, sexual, physical, or psychological abuse). Although the numbers reported with respect to sexual abuse remained insufficient to permit reliance on chi-square, Fisher's Exact Test, one tail = .500, indicated it was not significant. Quantitative analyses with respect to the remaining three types of abuse were permitted by the recoding of the respective variables. Statistical significance was not revealed with respect to any of the three abuse variables, verbal (chi-square = 1.11; d.f. = 1; p = .292), physical (chi-square = .045; d.f. = 1; p = .833), or psychological (chi-square = .051; d.f. = 1; p = .821) when nonviolent subjects (N = 45) and violent subjects (N = 45) were compared. With respect to verbal abuse, 44 percent of the nonviolent subjects reported abuse compared to 56 percent of the violent subjects. With respect to physical abuse, 47 percent of the nonviolent subjects reported abuse compared to 49 percent of the violent subjects. With respect to psychological abuse, 69 percent of the nonviolent subjects reported abuse compared to 67 percent of the violent subjects. Three nonviolent offenders (7 percent) and two violent offenders (4 percent) reported being sexually abused. Clearly, the comparative results of the Heide variables indicated that violent and nonviolent subjects had been nearly equally subjected to abuse.

Familial Dysfunction

It was expected that violent subjects would have experienced significantly greater exposure to familial dysfunction than nonviolent subjects. The three dysfunction variables (*documented, reported,* and *suspected*) were recoded to permit quantitative analyses. The recoded variables included two values: no dysfunction either documented, reported, or suspected; and dysfunction either documented, reported, or suspected.

Statistical significance was not revealed with respect to any of the three dysfunction variables, documented dysfunction (chi-square = 1.99; d.f. = 1; p = .158), reported dysfunction (chi-square = .002; d.f. = 1; p = .960), or suspected dysfunction (chi-square = .001; d.f. = 1; p = .981) when nonviolent subjects (N = 44) and violent subjects (N = 43) were compared. With respect to documented dysfunction, dysfunction was documented by 71 percent of the nonviolent subjects' case files compared to 57 percent of the violent subjects' case files. Eighty-two percent of both the nonviolent and violent subjects reported dysfunction. Likewise, with respect to both nonviolent and violent subjects, dysfunction was suspected in 95 percent of the subjects studied.

Familial Alcohol and Drug Abuse

Significance was not revealed when violent and nonviolent subjects were compared with respect to alcohol abuse but was revealed with respect to drug abuse by parental figures within the subjects' family of origin. The two variables addressing these issues were recoded to include two values: *no abuse* and *abuse of either substance.* After recoding, the reported numbers remained insufficient to permit quantitative analysis of the variable with respect to drug abuse using chi-square analysis, so Fisher's Exact Test, one tail, was used, revealing significant findings (p = .04). Only one (2 percent) of the violent subjects reported drug abuse by a parental figure, whereas seven (16 percent) of the nonviolent subjects reported such drug abuse. No statistical significance was revealed with respect to alcohol abuse by a parental figure (chi-square = .909; d.f. = 1; p = .340) when nonviolent subjects (N = 44) and violent subjects (N = 41) were compared. With respect to alcohol abuse by a parental figure, 51 percent of the violent subjects reported abuse compared to 40 percent of the nonviolent subjects.

Alcohol and Drug Use by Subject

The five variables with respect to substance use by the subject were recoded to include three values when nonviolent and violent subjects were compared. These values included *no substance use, occasional use of no more than twice monthly,* and *frequent use of once weekly to daily use.* The variables were recoded in this manner because some subjects described themselves as "weekend" substance users: substance users who refrained from alcohol and/or drugs during the week but reported heavy weekend use.

As depicted in table 5.8, the reported numbers with respect to heroin and LSD remained insufficient to permit quantitative analyses using available statistical measures. Ten percent of the nonviolent subjects reported frequent heroin use compared to 3 percent of the violent subjects. Three percent of the nonviolent subjects reported occasional heroin use. With respect to LSD use, 13 percent of the nonviolent subjects reported frequent use compared to 9 percent of the violent subjects. Occasional LSD use was reported by 6 percent of the violent subjects.

Statistical significance was not revealed with respect to marijuana use (chi-square = 4.684; d.f. = 2; p = .096) or cocaine use (chi-square = 1.383; d.f. = 2; p = .501) when nonviolent and violent subjects were compared. With respect to marijuana, 45 percent of the proportion of nonviolent subjects (N = 42) reported occasional use compared to 25 percent of the proportion of violent subjects (N = 44). Thirty-six percent of violent subjects reported frequent marijuana use compared to 33 percent of nonviolent subjects. With respect to cocaine, 19 percent of the violent subjects (N = 43) reported occasional use compared to 12 percent of nonviolent subjects (N = 42). Thirty-six percent of nonviolent subjects reported frequent cocaine use compared to 26 percent of violent subjects.

Statistical significance was revealed with respect to alcohol use (chi-square = 7.172; d.f. = 2; p = .028). A significantly greater proportion of violent subjects (51 percent; N = 45) than nonviolent subjects (31 percent; N = 45) reported frequent use. Furthermore, a significantly greater proportion of nonviolent subjects (40 percent) than violent subjects (16 percent) reported occasional alcohol use.

Table 5.8. Summary of Quantitative Analyses of Alcohol and Drug Use by Subject (in percentages)

	Nonviolent				Violent				
Category	No Use	Occasional Use	Frequent Use	N	No Use	Occasional Use	Frequent Use	N	Chi-Square Results
Alcohol	29	40	31	45	33	16	51	45	7.172; d.f. = 2; p = .028*
Marijuana	22	45	33	42	39	25	36	44	4.684; d.f. = 2; p = .096
Cocaine	52	12	36	42	56	19	26	43	1.383; d.f. = 2; p = .501
Heroin	87	3	10	40	97	0	3	36	**
LSD	87	0	13	38	85	6	9	34	**

Note: During interviews, subjects were queried with respect to alcohol and generalized drug use.

* Indicates significance

**Using chi-square, statistics not appropriate given N: Cells < 5

Psychological Evaluation of Subject

Two variables were included in this study to examine data with respect to psychological evaluation of the subjects. One of the variables was designed to quantitatively compare between the two subject groups the number of subject case files that contained psychological evaluations. The second variable was designed to extrapolate comparative qualitative data with respect to the evaluation outcomes.

Statistical significance was revealed with respect to the quantitative variable (chi-square = 10.370; d.f. = 1; p = .001) when nonviolent (N = 45) and violent subjects (N = 45) were compared. A significantly greater proportion of violent subjects' case files (34 percent) than nonviolent subjects' case files (7 percent) contained psychological evaluations. This finding was expected because the types of crimes committed by violent subjects were presumed to engender psychological evaluation more often than those of nonviolent subjects.

With respect to qualitative comparisons, only one of the nonviolent subject files contained a psychological evaluation. The evaluation indicated that the subject had an anger management problem. Ten of the violent subject files contained psychological evaluations. Two of the evaluations concluded that the subjects' evaluation results were in the *normal range*, two concluded that the subjects had an anger management problem, one concluded that the subject had a lack of inhibition, and five concluded that the subjects were sociopathic.

Age When Subject First in Trouble with the Law

A variable was developed to qualitatively compare age variations between nonviolent and violent subjects with respect to the subjects' first time in trouble with the law because quantitative statistics could not be appropriately done given the age distribution. Potential responses included *over 30, age 22–30, age 18–21, age 13–17, age 9–12,* and *age 5–8.*

Analogous patterns were shared by both groups of subjects with respect to the three categories of age 18–21, age 13–17, and age 9–12. Pattern differences were observed with respect to the two remaining age categories, age over 30 and age 22–30. A greater proportion of nonviolent subjects (22 percent) first encountered trouble with the law when over the age of 30 than the violent subjects (7 percent). In addition, a greater proportion of violent subjects (23 percent) first encountered trouble with the law when between the ages of 22 and 30 than did nonviolent subjects (5 percent).

With respect to both groups of subjects, the greatest proportion first encountered trouble with the law when they were between the ages of 13 and 17 (44 percent with respect to both groups). The latter finding was expected because the adolescent years for most people are a time of physical and emotional changes, some of which might be presumed to either encourage or inhibit criminal behavior.

Discussion of the Results

Cruelty to Animals Committed by Subject

The overall results of the study revealed compelling evidence to support the relationship of cruelty to animals and later violence against humans. Even when reported numbers with respect to some of the animal cruelty variables were insufficient to generate quantitative analyses (as in the case of the farm and stray animal variables), the qualitative findings suggested consistent and pronounced differences when the two groups of subjects were compared.

Pet Animals

Clearly the results with respect to cruelty committed to pet animals revealed both significant quantitative and qualitative findings when nonviolent and violent subjects were compared. Most of the cruel acts reported by violent subjects involved very young animals (e.g., puppies and kittens). Therefore, the animals targeted by the violent subjects were the types of animals that Mead (1964) concluded were particularly significant in view of the relationship of cruelty to animals and later violence against humans.

As noted, dogfighting was the only act of animal cruelty committed against pet animals reported by nonviolent subjects. With respect to dogfighting, additional qualitative findings are worthy of note. First, all three of the subjects indicated that the animals "were meant to fight" and that the animals wanted to fight. One of the three subjects precisely articulated that "it would have been cruel to stop a fight" because people often do so by forcing "a stick into the ear of the dog until it hurts." The second subject reported that one of his dogs, named Buster, was "a three-time champion," and he expressed pride that his dog had been "brave and tough." The third subject reported that he and his friends would never let the fight "get out of hand." They would bring their dogs to an open field where the dogfighting would take place. The subject commented that often the "older kids" who brought their dogs to the field to fight would "push for the fights to continue until dogs were hurt." The subject, however, reported that he and his friends had kept their dogs restrained on leashes so that the fights could be stopped. He also reported that he would bring peroxide with him to the fights to treat any bites or cuts that his dog sustained.

Dogfighting is unequivocally a form of animal cruelty. However, meaningful understanding of the relationship of cruelty to animals and later violence against humans requires an understanding of the qualitative meaning of the acts committed and the motives operational in their commitment. The subjects conceptualized dogfighting as representing those human qualities that their inner-city existences demanded of them, such as being tough, brave, and a winner.

Wild Animals

Wild animals was the only category of animals in this study in which analogous acts of cruelty had been committed by both nonviolent and violent offenders. Despite this fact, significant differences between the two groups were found with respect to the Ascione variables of frequency and empathy. In addition, the subject response variables revealed compelling qualitative differences when nonviolent and violent subjects were compared. The literature supporting a relationship between cruelty to animals and later violence against humans found the factors represented by these variables to be particularly important.

Farm Animals

Most of the subjects reported either urban or suburban backgrounds and had either no experience or limited exposure to farm animals. The low incidence of cruelty reported might be tied, at least in part, to this factor. Whereas wild animals such as birds and squirrels are frequently encountered even in urban environments, farm animals are usually limited to rural areas.

Despite the limited exposure to farm animals on the part of both the nonviolent and violent subjects, the qualitative findings with respect to the farm animal variables revealed significant distinctions between the two groups. In the case of farm animals, a conceptual process analogous to Lifton's (1986) *doubling* appeared to be operative in the perceptual framework of some of the nonviolent subjects in that they viewed the farm animals as pets. For example, one nonviolent subject reported that, when he was a young child, his father had slaughtered his pet pig, Oink Jackson, and that the subject had been allowed to see the "aftermath of the slaughter." Another nonviolent subject reported that his pet hog, Elizabeth, was also slaughtered for food. The subject reported that he was so upset by the incident that he ran away from home until he was found by his parents. He also reported that to this day he considers the slaughtering to have been a "cruel act" and that he "carries the sadness still." A third nonviolent subject reported that his father had killed his "pet chicken" for food and said that the incident had left a lasting impression. On a pragmatic level, all three subjects seemed aware that the ultimate fate of their pets was to be used as food. On a more intimate level, however, all three subjects expressed regret that the animals could not have been spared because they had also been pets. Only nonviolent offenders evidenced this conceptualization of a farm animal as a pet, as an animal that was given a name by the subject and treated with affection.

Stray Animals

The reported numbers with respect to cruelty committed against stray animals were often insufficient to test statistical significance. The category of stray animals, both in and of itself and in terms of cruelty committed, however, bears particular significance. As noted several times earlier, the literature supporting the relationship between cruelty to animals and later violence against humans has often concluded that cruelty committed against pet animals is especially significant. The term *stray* refers to dogs and cats, animals traditionally viewed as pet animals, that are homeless and thus devoid of human companionship and protection. Stray animals are often perceived by individual residents as "pests" and by societal officials (specifically with respect to municipal and county animal control policies) as "nuisance animals/throwaways," especially in the context of disease control (rabies, etc.). They are particularly vulnerable to the vagaries of existence on the street and are viewed by many people as being throwaway animals; millions of them are destroyed at animal shelters and animal control facilities in the United States each year. Four of the five violent subjects who reported acts of cruelty against stray animals reported frequent acts.

Stray animals, genetically coded to bond and coexist with humans, may by necessity revert to feral (or wild) behavior, but they are not wild animals. As a result, they often seek the company of humans for food and shelter. The trust that they frequently display toward humans can be dangerous. Some of the most horrific reports of animal cruelty either committed or observed by the subjects in this study involved stray animals. These reports included exploding animals by inserting fireworks into the animal's mouth or anus, using "Crazy Glue" to glue the paws of kittens and puppies to the middle of streets and then watching the animals be killed by passing cars, throwing stray animals to their death from rooftops, and setting animals on fire after drenching them in gasoline. Stray animals who are victims of cruelty can be analogized to the victims of serial killers, such as prostitutes and runaway juveniles; their deaths are often unseen and unknown by the average citizen until the remains are found.

Cruelty committed by the subject against stray animals, as in the case of all four animal categories, was recorded as such only if the subject clearly articulated that he had performed or participated in the act. Violent subjects reported many instances of observed cruelty to stray animals, which suggests complicity. Most of the observed acts reported by nonviolent subjects were vaguely described. Conversely, violent subjects described in detail many of the cruel acts they had observed, indicating that they had witnessed the cruelty throughout its duration. Even though these subjects may not have physically participated in the cruelty perpetrated, they may have participated psychologically. Kellert and Felthous (1985) concluded that one of the motives for animal cruelty is to enhance one's own aggressiveness. Many experts express a growing concern about the influence on children of violent video games and other violent entertainment (Heide, 1999); an analogous connection might be suggested here between some forms of observed animal cruelty and later committed violence. There is growing evidence that issues of passive versus active participation in animal cruelty should be conceptually addressed.

Ascione Variables

The results with respect to the Ascione variables were examined in detail earlier. The levels of significance represented by the Ascione *diversity/ cross* and *diversity/within* variables are especially noteworthy considering the comparatively high frequency of cruelty represented by the *nonviolent* subjects who had reported committed acts of cruelty against wild and pet animals (e.g., killing wild animals as a prelude to legitimate hunting or playing war games, and the confounding variable of dogfighting with respect to pet animals). Although the nonviolent subjects who had reported committed acts of cruelty to wild animals reported frequently committed acts, statistical significance was still revealed with respect to frequency when nonviolent and violent subjects were compared. Conversely, although statistical significance was not revealed with respect to frequency of cruelty committed to pet animals, the cruelty to pet animals reported by the nonviolent subjects was limited to dogfighting, an act the subjects did not perceive to be cruel.

Table 5.2 permits qualitative comparisons with respect to the most serious acts of cruelty committed by the two groups of subjects. This table does not show the total number of acts of cruelty committed by the subjects but only the most serious act committed by a given subject in each of the four animal categories. Although the only act of cruelty reported by the nonviolent subjects was *forced fighting* (dogfighting), several of the violent subjects reported that they had committed a variety of cruel acts, the most serious of which are indicated in table 5.2.

In summary, the conclusions of this study were based on rigorous methodological conceptualization and application. The quantitative and qualitative findings provide support for the relationship of cruelty to animals and later violence against humans.

Cruelty to Animals Observed by Subject

The findings with respect to observed animal cruelty reported by the subjects are conceptually tied to the Heide abuse results. Much of the literature cited in this study either concluded or suggested that exposure to violence in childhood, especially violence generated by familial environment, was a significant factor in later violence committed by the individual. Lockwood and Hodge (1998) included cruelty to animals as a significant component within this cycle of violence.

The study by Tapia (1971) concluded that the factor most often shared by subjects who had committed cruelty to animals was a chaotic home with aggressive parental models. Studies such as Tapia's have encouraged child and animal advocates alike to support the development of humane education programs both to enhance the development of empathy in children and to help identify children at risk. On the basis of the assumption that children exposed to domestic violence are at an elevated risk of eventually committing violence, many advocates view humane education as an applicable tool for violence intervention and prevention.

An interesting issue is raised with respect to the advocates themselves. Many advocates against violence have experienced violence. For example, many, if not most, of the organizations that have been established in this country to address victimization in its many forms have been founded by individuals who were victimized. These groups include advocacy and support groups for victims of drunk driving and sexual assault. Clearly, not all victims of violence go on to victimize others; many become victims' advocates.

Studies such as those by DeViney, Dickert, and Lockwood (1983) and Ascione (1998) strongly indicate that further research with respect to cruelty to animals and familial abuse is needed. DeViney et al. concluded that there were several parallels between the treatment of abused children and the treatment of pets within child-abusing families. Ascione's study concluded that violence in the family is the least escapable type of violence for a child. Furthermore, this research found that nearly a quarter of the subjects interviewed had reported that concern for their pets' welfare had prevented them from seeking shelter earlier. Ascione's findings suggest that many of the subjects loved their pets and risked their own safety because of them. Similarly, it might be assumed that many of the children of these subjects also loved their pets and empathized with them over the treatment afforded them by the abusers.

Clearly, the present study revealed that the majority of both nonviolent and violent subjects had endured some type of childhood abuse. Some of the subjects reported abuse that included the victimization of pets that had either been abused or killed by parental figures. On occasion, these subjects reported that they had attempted to intervene on behalf of their pets, such as by running away from home with the pet. Furthermore, these subjects had frequently expressed empathic feelings toward animals in general. Ultimately, despite the abusive backgrounds common to both groups of subjects, only the violent subjects went on to violently victimize others. Findings from this study suggest that *empathy* may be the fundamental factor operative with respect to those who choose violence and those who do not.

Heide Variables: Abuse and Dysfunction

Ultimately, the findings in this study with respect to abuse suggest some rather interesting implications. They appear to lend support to the findings of the study by Climent et al. (1972), which concluded that criminal behavior might be related to cultural factors, whereas violent behavior might be related to individual factors. This suggestion is based on the fact that childhood abuse was found to be prevalent among both nonviolent and violent subjects.

Factors such as poverty and abuse, and potentially a perceived alienation from the mainstream of society, may engender a culture that embraces criminality as its only recourse. Most of the nonviolent offenders who participated in this study described their criminal acts as a means to an end. The goal of their criminal acts was to acquire drugs to sustain a habit or to acquire money, status, and/or independence. Some of the subjects described their lives as a cycle of crime that they could not break. The choice between burglarizing an uninhabited house and invading a home and terrorizing, injuring, or murdering the victims may be an individual one. Obviously, violence is not an inevitable by-product of crime. Rather, it is a quantum leap in the continuum of the criminal's embrace of crime as a means to financial survival or reward. Most disturbingly, in the case of many violent subjects, violence appeared to be an end in itself.

Considering these results, a continuum with respect to familial dysfunction might be suggested. Given that there were substantially fewer documented instances of dysfunction than those reported and especially those suspected, it might be argued that the failure of others to identify, document, and intervene on behalf of families experiencing dysfunction permitted the dysfunction to continue and to adversely affect the development of all concerned. The result was the creation of a cycle of dysfunction that engendered in the next generation not only dysfunction but also criminal behavior and subsequent incarceration.

The fact that there were fewer instances of reported dysfunction than of suspected dysfunction, a variation of 13 percent, indicates that some subjects were not even aware of the dysfunction that affected their lives. Extrapolating from the findings of the study by Climent et al. (1972), it seems likely that a culture of dysfunction might be an important factor in the evolution of criminal behavior, particularly nonviolent criminal behavior, and that individual factors may be more involved in violent behavior.

Substance Use by Subject

Clearly, the study revealed that the majority of both nonviolent and violent subjects had reported substance use in one form or another. Consequently, further study is encouraged with respect to substance use and its relationship to criminal behavior. Some of the qualitative findings of this study suggest areas of inquiry. For example, many of the nonviolent subjects described their alcohol or drug use as a means to numb their pain. Although some of the violent subjects were self-medicating, others reported that substance use, particularly alcohol use, had been an influencing factor with respect to the violent crimes they had committed. In the case of some of the nonviolent subjects, substance use might have provided a temporary escape from pain or distress.For some of the violent subjects, substance use might have reduced inhibitions against violent tendencies or impulses. In such cases, substance use might have acted as a catalyst for violent behavior rather than as an escape.

In part III, we turn exclusively to qualitative analyses in an attempt to better understand our sample subjects. In-depth portraits are presented of violent offenders who appeared to graduate from acts of animal cruelty to human violence. Nonviolent offenders who committed or observed acts of cruelty are then discussed in the context of potential risk to hurting people.

Part Three

UNDERSTANDING THOSE WHO HURT ANIMALS: IN-DEPTH PORTRAITS

CHAPTER SIX

CASE STUDIES OF THREE THEORIES OF VIOLENT OFFENDERS

This section discusses cases from the study sample that exemplify the three theories of violent offenders presented in chapter 3: the Displaced Aggression Theory, the Sadistic Theory, and the Sexually Polymorphous Theory. These theories posit that individuals hurt animals and people to demonstrate anger and to vent anger toward innocent parties (Displaced Aggression Theory), to achieve pleasure from these violent activities and/or the reactions of others generated by their actions (Sadistic Theory), and to experience sexual excitement and release (Sexually Polymorphous Theory). It must be emphasized that these theories are tentative. The case examples are presented to stimulate further research.

Case Study: Displaced Aggression Offender

The offender was white and in his forties. He was serving multiple life sentences for a variety of violent crimes. The instant crimes were first-degree murder and kidnapping for ransom. Previously committed crimes included aggravated assault, rape, and kidnapping for ransom. The subject's victims included both males and females.

The subject stated that he was raised both by his natural parents and by adoptive parents. He reported that his natural parents were "drunks" and were "extremely violent with each other." Their arguments frequently escalated into physical altercations involving "guns, axes, anything they could get their hands on."

The subject related that, although he received "whoopings" from both his natural parents and his adoptive parents, the punishment that he received from his natural parents was "especially harsh" because they would beat him by using "whatever was around." He described his adoptive parents as "older"

129

and said they treated him well. The subject was the only child in the adoptive household, whereas he had shared the household of his natural parents with other siblings. He also indicated that his adoptive parents lived in spacious surroundings in a heavily wooded environment.

The subject related that, although he had very few friends, he had been an active participant in school activities, particularly in sports. He stated that he "never really spoke to anyone about any problems," that he preferred to go into the woods alone "to get away," and that he "never felt depressed." He reportedly had experimented with a wide variety of drugs, "including reefer, LSD, and speed," but maintained that it was alcohol that allowed him to do what he "probably would not have done otherwise." He indicated that, although he had "never discussed sexual matters while growing up" and his sexual experiences "had been limited to a few partners," the thought had occurred to him that he might be "sexually compulsive."

Records in the subject's case file noted that he left school in the ninth grade and that "he began a series of trips, hitch-hiking back and forth between Ohio and Florida." At the age of nineteen, he enlisted in the army. He was court-martialed three times for going AWOL (absent without leave) before he was discharged one year later. The subject's case file also contained a psychological evaluation that described him as "very dangerous because he is very [suggestible] and can be controlled by a strong personality to commit crimes" and diagnosed him as having a "sociopathic" personality. Examples of the subject's responses with respect to psychological screening that was administered to him included: (1) There are times "when I want to sleep but can't." (2) Many of my dreams are "about the woods." (3) Sex offenders are "misunderstood." (4) Death is "something strange." (5) Marriage is "for the birds." (6) Most men "don't like to work."

The subject reported that as an adolescent he had spent many hours in the woods with his hunting dogs "spear-hunting wild animals and stray dogs." He related that he "enjoyed the stalking and the overpowering of his prey" and that he "killed for the fun of it." He also admitted that sometimes he would allow his dogs to consume the prey.

The subject reported that at the age of sixteen, he returned to live for a time with his natural parents, and then with an older sister. Consistent with the subject's case file data, he stated that he joined the army at the age of nineteen, only to be discharged one year later. He indicated that his criminal history began during his brief tenure in the military, a statement that was validated by data in the case file. His crimes included assault and battery, vagrancy, and rape.

This subject appears to be an example of the *displaced aggression offender*. He described his natural parents as extremely violent with one another and with him. In addition, he did not choose to seek assistance or support from any source, such as from friends, a teacher, or a counselor. Rather, he seems to have chosen to channel his aggression by frequently going into the woods to stalk and kill his prey at close range (with a spear). Although the subject did not specifically cite anger as his motivation for killing, his choice of weapon certainly suggests aggressiveness. He reported that he always hunted with a spear, never a gun. This type of killing by its very nature is aggressively hands-on and lacks the potential distance and detachment made possible by the use of a firearm. Furthermore, he reported that, although he never hunted for food, he sometimes permitted his dogs to dismember and consume the animals he killed, something that he enjoyed observing.

The subject appears to have expressed his anger in this fashion from the age of twelve to sixteen. However, when he left his adoptive parents' home at the age of sixteen, he also left the outlet of the woods. He returned for a time to live with his natural parents, and then with an older sister. He described his natural parents' home as "small and with no real place to be alone." We suggest that his renewed relationship with his natural parents rekindled his unresolved anger toward them. Once he was removed from the buffer zone of the woods, his aggression escalated until it was redirected against humans; the escalation was triggered by his negative military experience.

The subject emphasized that his use of alcohol allowed him to do things that he otherwise would not have done. He also reported that he had never been successfully employed and that he did not like to work, hence his frequent AWOL status while in the army. He also stated that he suspected that he might be sexually compulsive. He committed his first crime of rape within a year of his departure from the military. We suggest that the subject raped because he considered himself unable to attract and sustain conventional sexual relationships because of his low social and economic standing. Furthermore, his instant crimes of kidnapping, rape, and murder were committed within the context of ransom demands; his criminal acts were committed within the context of his consistent failure to achieve personal or financial success.

The subject's failure to cope with the financial and personal demands of life may have engendered acute anger directed at those whom he considered to be successful and empowered. This anger was cumulative, compounding the anger that was initially fueled by the violence he was exposed to as a child. The subject's use of alcohol and drugs was the catalyst that facilitated the commission of his violent acts. As if to come full circle, he ultimately murdered his victims by stabbing them; he then concealed their bodies by dragging them deep into the woods, in the same place where he had stalked and killed animals when a child.

Case Study: Sadistic Offender

The offender was black and in his thirties. He requested that he be addressed by his self-proclaimed biblical name and reported that he was fervently devoted to Yahweh. The subject stated that he was a high school graduate, but that he was a slow learner owing to a learning disability. He indicated that he was essentially self-taught and very knowledgeable about history, slavery, and the Bible. The subject was extremely articulate. He interspersed his personal background reporting with historical facts and quotes from the Bible. He said that he wanted his story "to be broadcast around the world."

The subject said that he was serving a life sentence. Records in his case file indicated that he had an extensive criminal history including robbery, battery on law enforcement officer, domestic violence, and tampering with evidence. The subject's instant offenses were arson, willful damage to a structure, and murder. The case file reported that the subject's victim died of burns sustained when the victim's car was set on fire. The adjacent building was also partially destroyed.

The subject made various racist remarks yet also reported that "we should love" and that "harmony can result when we realize that we are all the same blood and mind." He maintained that God is a "God of opposites," and the subject's mind-set appeared to repeatedly alternate between expressed tolerance and retribution.

The subject reported that 85 percent of blacks are illiterate because whites want to keep them that way and said that "whites took control of the planet from a log cabin." He maintained that he was influenced by "a corrupt America" but that "evil will be destroyed and the righteous will take out the wicked" by various means "such as by car accidents and other tragedies" and that "something may fall out of the sky."

The subject described his life as "hell with temporary pleasure." He reported that his natural father was "killed by the police" when the subject was seven years old and that his stepfather "was hell." He said that his stepfather was cruel "in a way deeper than physical" and "that his mother disciplined in a way she thought was right, with a rod of discipline that was not physical." He maintained that he had "very little childhood and had to grow up fast." He said that his stepfather was a "heavy drinker and a gambler" and that the family was "poverty-stricken." He related that, as a result, he was on his own from a young age and that he "sold drugs to get by."

The subject was very verbal, yet evasive, with respect to his views on animals and his past experiences with them. His evasiveness was interesting, considering the detail with which he discussed other topics. He appeared to be intentionally inconclusive, despite the fact that he clearly articulated that he had both committed and observed numerous cruel acts against animals. He also appeared to enjoy relating the limited details that he did share. The subject expressed no remorse and spoke of the animals as if they were inanimate objects. He reported that he "had been mean to animals" but that once "fed wickedness, one becomes wicked." He described his cruelty to animals as "small pranks that killed them." He indicated that his cruelty to animals "involved mostly cats, but included other animals, too." He suspected that many of these animals were pets and described pet animals as "very negative" and "tamed like inmates." He appeared to disdain pet animals for the same qualities that endear them to most other people. The subject reported no experiences with respect to wild animals. He described farm animals as "unholy because they are domesticated" and said that "to touch a swine brings injury to the body."

The subject did not accept responsibility either for his crimes against humans or for the cruelty to animals that he had committed. Rather, he blamed such external forces as television and reported that "once you see it, you mimic it, you act it." He described the cruel acts that he had committed against animals as "all part of the same dynamics."

This subject appears to be an example of a *sadistic offender*. According to the case file, the subject's crime against his victim resulted in tremendous suffering. Most of the victim's body sustained third-degree burns, but the victim did not die outright. Yet, rather than expressing remorse, the subject dispassionately reported that the wicked, such as he perceived his victim to be, would be punished by ways such as "car *accidents.*" Similarly, as previously cited, he described his cruelty to animals as "*small pranks* that killed them." He appeared to enjoy relating both his philosophy and the facts of his crimes and cruelty. Clearly, the subject committed both violent acts against humans and acts of cruelty against animals that were intended to cause suffering. Furthermore, his description of these acts as "accidents" and "small pranks" revealed a cavalier and sadistic attitude.

Case Study: Sexually Polymorphous Offender

The offender, a high school graduate, was black and in his forties. He had been incarcerated for approximately fifteen years for armed burglary and sexual battery when interviewed. According to the case file, the state attorney's office suspected that the subject had been involved in seventeen to twenty rapes. The court report characterized the instant offense as "a most heinous crime." The police report indicated that "the defendant terrorized his victim and, during the course of the offense, he held a knife to the victim's throat and cut her." The report noted that "the victim requested immediate notification if this man ever escapes or is released." The results of a psychological evaluation concluded that the subject was "not actively psychotic."

The subject reported that his parents were divorced when he was eleven years old and that his mother never remarried, but that his father did twice. He characterized his mother as "affectionate" but indicated she had "a stubborn streak." He described his father as a minister who was very strict and who set high standards. The subject reported that he "never saw" his father after the divorce.

The subject reported data consistent with psychological abuse. He appeared to have received many inconsistent and ambivalent messages from his mother with respect to affection. He stated that his mother would "insult and curse" at him when she was disappointed in him. She would express dissatisfaction with his accomplishments when he "did something wrong." He also said that his mother would punish him "with a paddle or belt," data consistent with physical abuse.

The subject reported that he mostly dealt with his problems "alone" and that he had "many associates, but few friends." He indicated that he had experienced his "share of conflicts," some with strangers and some with people that he knew. The subject related that, although he was "no Don Juan," he "had many sexual partners." He denied any sexual compulsions. He had never married and had no children.

The subject related that during adolescence he had hunted rabbits, birds, and other small wild animals "just as something to do." He had observed "neighborhood people throw potash on dogs a few times," which resulted in the dogs being "badly burned." The subject described the latter as "disgusting to see" but said that he had "no personal feelings" about it. He recalled that he had "once mistreated a little puppy" but could not remember what he did, only that he "knew it was bad." The incident took place at his father's house, and the subject told his father that the puppy "ran away."

This subject appears to be a *sexually polymorphous offender,* meaning that he could attain sexual release only through violence. The Sexually Polymorphous Theory proposes that sexual and aggressive tendencies become developmentally fused as a result of childhood experiences. The subject clearly indicated numerous contradictory perceptions and feelings about his mother during his developmental years. His mother's behavior toward him reportedly had alternated between demonstrations of affection and cruelty, and the subject did not appear to be able to distinguish affectionate from abusive treatment. His statements about sexual matters also indicated contradictory perceptions. The subject referred to himself as "no Don Juan," and yet he reported that he had experienced many sexual partners. Furthermore, despite his reportedly frequent sexual encounters, the subject reported no data indicating that he had experienced at any time a meaningful or lasting relationship with a woman. He had never married, and he had no children.

As previously noted, the subject's father had been a minister. The subject reported that neither smoking nor drinking had been tolerated in the household. Given the strictness of the father's standards, it might be presumed that the father's teachings and expectations with respect to sexual matters were equally strict. Within this context, it might be suggested that the subject's perceptions with respect to sexual matters were significantly influenced during his formative years by his father, even though he did not see his father after his parents divorced. The findings of Wax and Haddox (1974), however, would suggest that the father would likely have remained a viable influence during the subject's developmental years. In this view, as the subject sexually matured, he might have developed conflicts with respect to sexual issues. This sexual confusion might have been compounded by the contradictory emotional messages from his mother.

The subject's crime of sexual battery was accompanied by excessive psychological and physical aggression. According to the police and court reports, the victim was terrorized, raped, and physically attacked. As noted, the state attorney's office suspected that the subject was a "serial rapist." Clearly, it appeared from the data available that the subject experienced sexual arousal while simultaneously expressing aggression. It did not appear that he harbored conscious aggression toward any particular person, such as his mother. Rather, it appeared that the subject's sexual and aggressive impulses had become fused within the course of his personality development and that they could not be separated.

In the next chapter, we look closely at six cases of nonviolent offenders. Some of these offenders committed acts of animal cruelty as children and yet seem at little risk of hurting people. Some who observed animal cruelty as children seem at low risk of acting violently toward human beings whereas others seem at higher risk. What appears to make the difference?

NONVIOLENT OFFENDERS INVESTIGATED

An in-depth look at the cases of nonviolent subjects provides important insights. This chapter presents six case studies of nonviolent subjects. Cases one and two admitted that they had committed acts of cruelty but did not seem at risk for hurting human beings as adults. Cases three through six committed no acts of cruelty, although all four had observed acts of animal cruelty. Cases three and four seemed at very low risk for hurting people in the future. In contrast, cases five and six seemed at high risk for hurting human beings in the future. These six case examples of nonviolent offenders, like the examples of violent offenders in the previous chapter, are presented to stimulate future research.

Cruelty to Animals: Acts Committed

The results of this study indicated that nonviolent subjects, although to a significantly lesser degree then violent subjects, committed acts of cruelty to animals. These findings suggest that the identification and understanding of the factors operative in the cases of nonviolent subjects who committed cruelty to animals might contribute to a greater understanding of the phenomenon as a whole.

Case Study One

The subject was a thirty-nine-year-old black man. He had been sentenced as a habitual felony offender and had served five years of a thirty-year sentence. His instant offense was sale or purchase of cocaine. All of the subject's past offenses were either drug or property related. Although he had a high school diploma, he claimed that he was not successful in school past the second grade owing to a complete lack of motivation. At the time of the interview, he had just completed a paralegal course at the institution. The subject, who had never been married, reported that he had been a drug addict for the past twenty years, using "everything they make," because he was "lonely."

He said that his mother was fifteen years old when she gave birth to him. The subject said that his mother was "more like a sister" and that she provided "no real parenting." He indicated that his natural father had been an alcoholic and that he had no contact with his father until he was fifteen years of age. He described himself as a "spoiled brat" who always got what he wanted. He recalled that he was indulged not only by his mother but also by his grandmother and his "auntie." He stated that his mother was "too slack" and that he "took everything for granted." He described himself as a "good athlete" in school and "the class clown." He related that he was popular with his peers and described himself as "the leader of the pack."

The subject reported that, when he was eleven years old, he witnessed his mother murder her boyfriend. The murder was also recorded in the subject's case file. The subject recalled that from that time until he was fifteen, he lived with his grandmother. Thereafter, he raised himself.

The subject related that, now that he was in prison, he "had time to reflect." He maintained that he "never hurt nobody." His case file indicated that he had recently been disciplined for "stealing six chicken omelet sandwiches and twenty-eight packets of sugar." The subject stated that when he was between eight and ten years of age, he shot raccoons with a BB gun "just to do it." He indicated that he outgrew this behavior and that, as an adult, he has no interest in hunting or any outdoor activities and he would never go "where there's no motel." The subject had very limited experience with farm animals and reported only that he was "chased by a rooster once" when he was a little boy. He recalled having many pets as a child, including guinea pigs and hamsters. He said that, while he loved dogs, a pet dog "had better do the job" of being a good protector or he would take it "to the SPCA," so that someone else could have it. The subject reported that he knew of some neighborhood kids "who would hurt strays" but had never observed any cruelty committed.

The cruelty to wild animals that the subject reported might have been the result of *displaced aggression*. He related that he had committed cruelty to wild animals (raccoons) when he was eight to ten years of age, during which time his mother was involved in the violent relationship he described. The subject engaged in no acts of cruelty to animals after the death of the mother's boyfriend. Therefore, it might be argued that the subject's anger was defused by the cessation of the domestic violence to which he had been exposed. Obviously, it might also be argued that the violence he observed (i.e., witnessing the boyfriend's murder by the mother) might have been expected to trigger, rather than defuse, his inclination to commit continued acts of cruelty to animals.

Five factors might have prevented the continuation of such behavior. First, the mother's arrest and subsequent incarceration removed the subject from his highly dysfunctional domestic environment. Second, the subject reported no information that indicated either that he was deeply bonded to his mother or that he missed her after her arrest. Therefore, although he may have indeed been traumatized by the murder he witnessed and the fact that it was his mother who perpetrated the crime, he did not appear to be traumatized by his mother's arrest and her removal from his life. Rather, extrapolating from the data provided by the subject with respect to his mother, it might be more accurate to suggest that he was traumatized not by the removal of his mother, the person, from his life, but rather by the realization that he had never enjoyed the loving and nurturing relationship represented in his mind by mother, the concept, in his life. Third, although the subject was academically unsuccessful in school, he reported that he had many friends and was socially popular. This factor may have given him a positive outlet to help balance the effects of the trauma that he sustained as a result of the murder. The fourth factor involves the subject's reported fondness for animals, particularly for pet animals. This factor may have tempered any inclination toward continued cruelty that he might otherwise have experienced. The fifth factor might have involved the subject's reported use of drugs, which by his own admission served as an escape from his loneliness.

Case Study Two

The subject, a thirty-eight-year-old black man, was sentenced as a habitual felony offender and was serving a thirty-year sentence for burglary of an unoccupied dwelling. Past offenses included both drug and property offenses. The subject reported that he was never academically successful and that he dropped out of school in the eighth grade and subsequently earned a GED. He had never married but was the father of a fifteen-year-old child whom he had not seen since the child was two years of age. The subject described himself as a "recovering addict." He reported that he originally turned to drugs "to mask the pain and to fit in" and that he sometimes experienced "suicidal thoughts."

The subject described his childhood familial situation as "hard to explain." He related that he was raised by grandparents on their farm and that he did not know his natural mother until he was five years of age. He had a brief acquaintance with his natural father when he was nine years old, but that a relationship was neither developed nor sustained. He stated that a bitter custody fight took place between his grandparents and his natural mother and that his mother ultimately won custody. He reported that his "granddaddy," of whom he spoke affectionately, died two years later. The subject said that he had four siblings but that two had died tragic deaths; "one had drowned and one had been stabbed to death."

The subject reported that his mother had remarried and that she and the stepfather were alcoholics. He said that his natural mother never communicated with him and never showed affection. His stepfather was similarly uninvolved with him but "provided financially" for the family. He recalled that the stepfather was very violent and regularly beat his mother and the children. The subject described the stepfather as "cruel" and recalled an incident in which the stepfather tied the subject's brother to a tree and beat him severely.

On several occasions he ran away from home, and he was placed for a time in a foster home. The subject said of living in the foster home that it "was bad there, too" and that he had been the only black child there. At the age of fifteen, he reportedly dropped out of school, lived on the streets, and started getting into drugs and trouble with the law.

The subject related a childhood incident involving a pig that left a lasting impression. He reported that his grandfather took him hunting from time to time, and when the subject was eight years old, the grandfather gave him a rifle as a birthday gift. He stated that until that point, he had only used a BB gun, and he wanted to see what a "real gun" could do. He shot and killed a neighbor's pig. The grandfather was very upset about the incident and broke the subject's rifle. In addition, the grandfather arranged with the neighbor for the subject to work for the neighbor for a period of one year to compensate for the deed. The subject described the punishment as "like doing community service." He indicated that, although he resented the work at first, he came to enjoy working around the pigs and that he grew "especially fond of the baby pigs."

This incident was the only act of cruelty to animals that the subject reported committing. It appears that the grandfather's response to the cruelty was a critical factor in preventing further acts of cruelty. This position is based on Mead's warning that "a failure of punishment here, when there is a cultural reliance on teaching and learning, can be as fatal or possibly even more fatal, than too violent punishment" (1964, p. 21).

Clearly, the grandfather's punishment was not intended to hurt the subject. He was neither physically beaten nor psychologically humiliated. Instead, the grandfather demanded that the boy compensate for his cruel act in a positive manner that was directly tied to the transgression. In addition, the arrangement was made by the only family member who was loved and trusted by the subject. Furthermore, the compensation also served as a means for the subject to develop empathy for the type of animal that he had victimized, and it is apparent that empathy did indeed develop. The subject reported the details of an act of cruelty that he witnessed subsequently. He recalled that, when he was nine years old, his stepfather tied a goat to a tree and slaughtered it by cutting the animal's throat. The subject related that the goat "was screaming, like he was crying" and died a "slow and cruel death"; the incident left a strong and troubling impression.

Cruelty Observed: Low-Risk Nonviolent Subjects

Some of the literature about the relationship of cruelty to animals and later violence against humans has suggested that cruelty to animals is one of several symptomatic manifestations that often appear in the behavior of individuals who have been exposed to familial abuse and violence. The results of this study revealed that the majority of both the nonviolent and violent subjects surveyed reported abuse. The following two case studies provide qualitative data with respect to nonviolent subjects who did not report acts of cruelty committed to animals. Suggestions are offered as to why these subjects chose not to abuse animals.

Case Study Three

The subject, a twenty-five-year-old white man, was sentenced as a habitual felony offender and was serving a life sentence. The subject's instant offense was introducing a contraband substance within a correctional facility; his previous crimes were property and drug related.

The subject had numerous convictions beginning at age sixteen. He dropped out of school in the ninth grade and subsequently earned a GED and some college credits in business administration. According to his case file, he successfully completed a variety of vocational courses, including plumbing, masonry, and carpentry.

The subject reported that he has only seen his natural father on two occasions, once when the subject was five years old and again when he was fifteen. He had brothers and sisters from the same father but from different mothers. He also had brothers and sisters from the same mother but from different fathers. He related that these various fathers, including his natural father, were all "crack-heads." He lived with his natural mother, and, although they "got along fairly well," the two had "very little in common." The subject stated that he received inadequate parenting because his mother was always working. He recalled that both he and an older brother shared most of the household responsibilities and that it was like "the blind leading the blind."

He said that his mother was "on drugs all the time" and that he was the victim of both sexual and physical abuse by his mother. He reported that his mother "believed in the belt" and that "she could live without a man." He indicated that his mother "kept her sex with men private, but when she was on cocaine, she would exploit her nudity" and she would fondle the subject and his brother. The sexual abuse continued until he was thirteen or fourteen years old, at which time he often ran away from home to avoid it.

The subject stated that on one occasion, his mother held a knife to his throat and threatened to kill him because he prematurely ate a piece of birthday cake. His brother intervened and begged his mother to stop. It bothered the subject that his mother never apologized for the act. He indicated "that so many things come back" and that he was reflecting on his life for the first time.

The subject reported that he began committing crime at a young age, although he "knew right from wrong." He maintained that "most people commit crimes because they want to have what they otherwise can't, and that the attraction is very strong." He stated that his father never allowed him or his brother "to be kids" and that the two boys "had to work to eat." He was still appealing through the courts because he did not believe that "justice had really been done." He stated that he had "never been violent and had never harmed anyone." Furthermore, he related that he was becoming more "self-aware" and was attempting to better understand his past.

The subject enjoyed outdoor activities and "the peace of mind and freedom" that they provide. He had never hunted, and he reported no acts of cruelty committed to wild animals. He stated that he never intentionally hurt or killed an animal and that he "had been a vegetarian on and off, but that the chow hall has nothing but meat." He recalled that he had observed the slaughtering of farm animals at his uncle's ranch and that he was aware that farm animals were administered antibiotics and other chemicals that are unhealthy to humans. He said that "goats can detect their death, and they cry."

The subject reported an incident involving an animal that revealed parental abuse. When he was eleven years old, his mother directed him to bring some fish to the yard and to leave it there for the pet cat. The family puppy ate the fish instead. Unlike the digestive system of a dog, the digestive system of a cat is designed to tolerate bones. Neither his mother nor the man with whom she was presently living intervened by taking the puppy to a veterinarian. As a result, the puppy died an agonizing death. The subject reported that he was blamed for the death, beaten, and forced to bury the puppy.

Clearly, the subject was the victim of pervasive parental abuse. However, he appeared to be introspective and was able to empathize with the pain and misfortune of others, particularly animals. He maintained that neither he nor his brother had ever hurt anyone despite the abuse they both sustained. The empathy displayed by the subject appeared to be a critical factor in his nonviolent behavior. The puppy's death from ingesting the fish appeared to have left a very strong impression on him. The subject did not emphasize the fact that he was blamed for the death and punished. Rather, he emphasized the pain that the animal experienced and the fact that no adult had intervened to help the suffering animal. He appeared most disturbed by the fact that the animal could have been helped and was not. Perhaps he identified with the puppy and that identification engendered empathy that, in turn, engendered compassion.

Case Study Four

The subject, a thirty-eight-year-old Hispanic man, was serving a term of forty years and had been sentenced as a habitual felony offender. His instant offense was trafficking in stolen property. The subject's past offenses included burglary of an unoccupied structure and grand theft.

The subject reported that he had just recently been divorced. He had been married for seven years and was the father of two children. He was born in Puerto Rico but came to the United States as a young boy. He had traveled to Puerto Rico several times in past years to visit family and his seven horses that lived on a family member's farm.

The subject related that his father abandoned the family when he was five years old. He stated that his mother "is everything." She had visited him a week prior to the interview, and they remain close. His mother took care of him and his siblings as best she could, but the family went on welfare after the father left.

The subject described his father as a "macho man" who had another wife even when he was still living with the subject's mother and her children. He reported that his father had been physically abusive to his mother and would "beat her up." He characterized his father as a harsh disciplinarian who would punish the children "with the first thing that came into his hand." He indicated that his father had been an alcoholic, "but that you can't blame all of it on alcohol." The subject added that "some things cannot be forgiven; it just hurts." The man's father hated his brother "because his skin is dark," and, therefore, the father "insisted that the boy cannot be his son." His mother had relationships with three men during the years after his natural father left, but none resulted in marriage.

The subject recalled that he was placed in a special school because the system thought he "was loose in the head." He "got into serious trouble at a young age like stealing cars, breaking into peoples' houses, and smoking weed." The subject maintained that he "did everything" but that he had never hurt anyone.

He said that he attended church three to four times a week but that he did not talk about his faith and did not consider himself a "religious person." He related that "some guys walk around with a Bible all the time and they don't live anything they preach."

The subject reported that, although he could give up drugs each time he was "locked up," he could not resist drugs when he was on the outside. He had a daily "crack habit" prior to his most recent arrest and incarceration.

He indicated that he loved horses; he had the name of his favorite horse, Josefina, tattooed on his arm. He stated that he used to "break horses" and that "if you treat a horse right, he will be good." He said that the treatment of animals on farms, in general, was often cruel. The subject reported, for example, that "to take away a calf from its mother and to use it as veal was as cruel as taking a human baby away from its mother after she has endured the suffering of labor."

He described his father as "cruel" to animals. He reported that his father would slaughter horses by "hitting them with a two-by-four and then sticking them in the heart until the horse slowly died." The subject maintained that animals "want to live just like us." He also described how his father killed the subject's pet chicken, which "used to sleep in the front of the house and was too fat to fly into a tree." His father "just killed it" and "wasted the meat and didn't care."

The subject also reported that when a neighbor's dog ate two of his father's chickens, the father retaliated by feeding the dog a crushed light-bulb concealed in food. The dog died a very painful death because the glass "cut his guts up." The subject maintained that his father "now suffers for all the pain he caused because he is very sick now."

Clearly, the subject had never successfully coped with life outside prison, and he admitted that he had turned to drugs whenever he was released. However, although he had an extensive criminal record, the subject had never committed a violent crime and reportedly did not feel safe within the prison "because there are psychos and violence here." The subject's reported compassion for animals and empathy toward their circumstances appeared to be a crucial factor with respect to his nonviolence.

The Red Flag: Nonviolent Subjects at Risk

Remarks made by two of the nonviolent subjects raised a red flag of concern, despite that fact that their criminal histories contained no violent crimes. Both subjects were young and appeared to be fascinated with violence. In addition, they reported many detailed instances of observed cruelty to animals.

Case Study Five

The subject was an eighteen-year-old white man. He was a first-time offender serving a four-year sentence for burglary and grand theft.

The subject's case file indicated that he had been expelled from school in the tenth grade for truancy and had been a heavy drug user. His "primary drug was cocaine, which he had inhaled 1–2 times weekly since the age of 12." The subject reported that heavy drug use was responsible for his crimes.

He related that his natural father died when the subject was five years old. His father was hit by a car and stayed in a coma for five years. "When gangrene set in," his mother "pulled the plug." The subject was very angry after his father's death and "had a lot of aggression." Two years later his natural mother died after suffering a heart attack in the shower. He described his mother as being all he had.

The subject was adopted by an older sister after his mother's death. He did not get along with his sister, because his sister, unlike his mother, who "didn't have lots of rules," was "tough." He started "hanging around friends at a chop shop" and experimented with a variety of drugs, including "acid, weed, heroin, and cocaine." He described himself as "quiet and laid-back, but when someone messes with me there's no telling what I am capable of." The subject related that he was a gang member and that "people are threatened by me." He described his fellow gang members as "into drugs and retaliation" and his crimes as "a relief from boredom and a thrill."

The subject described prison life as "filled with homosexual stuff and fights." He indicated that most of his friends were "older Hispanics" and that he preferred the company of adults who could teach him to look out for himself. The subject reported that he had been in close management numerous times and that no one could make him do what he did not want to do.

He had observed many acts of cruelty to animals. He "would get high" and watch his friends "do crazy things, like super-gluing cats to the road and then watching them get run over, and throwing animals off roofs." He had also watched his friends "beat up bums," which he described as a "thrill to watch."

The subject reported that he visited a farm once on a school field trip but that it "left no impression." He had owned many pets including a Great Dane, Japanese fighting fish, a tarantula, ferrets, and an iguana. He did not elaborate as to his feelings for any of the pets mentioned and did not mention any of the pets by name. He reported no experiences with wild animals.

The subject boasted extensively about his friends' violent activities, which included drive-by shootings and attacks on tourists. He appeared to be fascinated with the lifestyles of these friends.

It is possible that this subject might be in a transitional stage leading toward violence. He repeatedly reported that he was aggressive and that the cruelty to animals and violence toward people that he had observed were thrilling. Clearly, he was not a casual observer of these acts but observed them by choice and by design. The committed acts were undoubtedly cruel and appeared to be fueled by sadistic impulses, and, alarmingly, the subject enjoyed watching them.

Case Study Six

The subject was twenty-one years old and white; he was serving an eight-year sentence for grand theft auto. He reported that he was divorced and the father of one child but that he no longer had contact with his former wife or his child. The subject's case file indicated that he left school in the ninth grade and was working toward a GED. According to the file, the subject was on a waiting list for stress- and anger-management classes.

The subject related that his natural father died when he was six years old. Despite his father's death, the family remained financially solvent because his mother was a factory manager. His mother remarried twice after his father's death, but both marriages ended in divorce. He described his mother as "tough" but said that "communication was always open."

The subject had one brother and one sister. He described the difference between his brother and himself as "the difference between day and night." He reported that, although his brother had also served time, his brother's incarceration had been a "misfortune."

The subject stated that he had had many sexual partners and that he became sexually active at the age of nine or ten. His first encounter with the law took place when he was eleven years old. He was placed in an alternative school "but got kicked out of there, too." The subject said that he lived basically on his own from the age of thirteen and that he "lived a dangerous lifestyle." He maintained that he "felt safe on the streets, but made enemies." He described himself as a "highly rebellious teenager who got into the wrong crowd." The subject reported that he experimented with a variety of drugs, including marijuana, LSD, and cocaine. He saw himself as an addict who "would never be cured, but was recovering."

The subject reported that he would often accompany one of his former stepfathers, who was an avid sport hunter. The subject had no experiences with farm animals. He had "owned dogs" from time to time.

The subject reported that he had observed numerous acts of cruelty to neighborhood animals that he "assumed were pets." He had observed his friends set animals on fire and "stick firecrackers in the mouths of animals, and light them." He "didn't give much thought" to these acts and "had no feelings" about them. Clearly, the subject felt no empathy toward these animals, which had undoubtedly suffered.

This subject might also be in a transitional stage leaning toward violence. He did not express any close familial attachments or emotions, even as far as his child was concerned. He appeared fascinated with his previous "life on the streets" and the danger associated with it. He became animated when he discussed this aspect of his life and consistently attempted to convey a tough-guy attitude. The subject was in the process of having tattoos of skulls, located on his forearms, changed to dragons. He gave no indication that he intended to take up a legitimate lifestyle upon release from prison.

A blueprint for ending senseless pain and destruction is presented in the final part of this book. Following a brief summary of the study, we focus on conclusions that can be drawn and make recommendations for further research.

Part Four

A BLUEPRINT TO END SENSELESS PAIN AND DESTRUCTION

SUMMARY, CONCLUSIONS, AND RECOMMENDATIONS

This study was designed to examine the relationship of cruelty to animals and later violence against humans. Previous studies have suggested that cruelty to animals might indeed be a viable link to interpersonal violence (see, e.g., Arluke & Lockwood, 1997; Ascione, 1999; Flynn, 1999). Furthermore, these studies concluded that further research was necessary and served to stimulate this study.

Cruelty to animals has long served as a red flag in law enforcement circles with respect to extremely violent offenders. The extensive literature on serial killers, for example, has often cited cruelty to animals as a precursor to the violence later targeted against human victims. Furthermore, some of the recent literature with respect to domestic violence has cited cruelty to animals as part of an insidious cycle of violence that victimizes families. Cruelty to pet animals has been regarded as a barometer of familial abuse. In addition, pet animals, which often are loved and treated like children in our culture, have been viewed as victims in their own right. Therefore, many advocates of children and animals have come to see cruelty to animals as a serious matter because of the analogous human victimization it often represents (Lockwood & Hodge, 1997).

The overall results of the present retrospective study of adult offenders support previous research efforts indicating a relationship between cruelty to animals committed during childhood and later violence perpetrated against humans. The null hypothesis, which stated that there would be no statistically significant difference between the proportion of violent offenders who had committed past acts of cruelty to animals and the proportion of nonviolent offenders who had committed past acts of cruelty to animals, was rejected. The findings indicate that violent offenders who committed crimes as adults were significantly more likely than nonviolent offenders to have committed acts of cruelty against animals in general, and pet and stray animals in particular, as children. Even when reported numbers for some of the animal cruelty variables used in this study were insufficient to yield statistical significance (as in the case of the farm and wild animal variables), the qualitative findings derived from these variables suggested consistent and pronounced differences when the two groups of subjects were compared.

Clearly, the qualitative results of this study, as well as the quantitative findings, both stimulate and provide direction for further inquiry. Limitations in this study need to be addressed in future research. The number of sample subjects restricted the types of analyses that could be completed on a number of occasions, and in some cases may have masked significant findings. For example, differences between the two offender groups regarding cruelty to farm and wild animals just missed the level of significance. In this study we noted the tendency toward significance; it is likely that a larger sample size would have allowed for a better test of these relationships and more definitive results.

In addition to increasing sample size, this study needs to be replicated in other prison settings. The study looked for differences in acts of childhood animal cruelty among violent and nonviolent inmates in one maximum-security prison in Florida. It is unknown whether the significant differences between these two offender groups in terms of cruelty to animals in general, and pet and stray animals specifically, would hold up in other prison settings across the country.

It is important to note that the population used in this study is a restrictive one. One could ask, Why should one believe the reports of convicted felons? We believe that several factors in our study helped us obtain valid data. Our in-depth interviews, which lasted from forty-five minutes to over two hours, allowed for rapport to build between the interviewer and the offender and enabled us to detect inconsistencies either during the report or upon listening to the taped interviews. The setting was conducive to open dialogue; the interviews took place in a private room and were not supervised or monitored by correctional officers. In addition, the inmates were told that the interviewer was not connected with the prison and that reports would be considered confidential and would not be tied to them in any way. It was clear, given the independence of the study, that information the inmates provided would not help them or hurt them in terms of their sentence length. Moreover, our access to correctional files allowed us to verify offense history and available data on demographic and social history. These corroborative data increased our confidence that the information reported to us by the offenders was likely an accurate representation of their perceptions and memories of events. We noted in our reporting when offender statements, affect, demeanor, or corroborative data did not add up, and we made coding decisions to reflect these inconsistencies. Thus, while we feel confident overall about the data reported to us and the coding decisions we made, which we discussed in pertinent sections, we see great value in further testing with other populations the relationship between childhood animal cruelty and violence against people.

Would the association of animal cruelty and human violence hold up if tested in a noninstitutionalized sample? If we focus on nonlethal violence, is it likely that most individuals who commit violence against people are not prosecuted, let alone convicted and sentenced to prison. Would the correlation found in this research be replicated if the research were conducted in the general population; that is, would acts of cruelty to animals distinguish "free-world people" who are violent toward human beings from those who are not?

These findings raise an even more fundamental question, one that increasingly demands an answer as more studies show a correlation between animal cruelty and subsequent violence toward people: Is aggression against animals committed by children *predictive* of subsequent adult aggression against human beings? Our results underscore the need for a longitudinal study of children through their adult years to see to what extent childhood violence toward specific types of animals is causally connected to adult violence against humans.

This study found that cruelty to animals is a complex phenomenon. It reinforced the idea that any meaningful inquiry into its dynamics requires the application of rigorous methodological standards and conceptual precision. The results of this study have implications with respect to the phenomenon of cruelty to animals and its relationship to human violence. The motivations for cruelty to animals are as diverse and complicated as those for interpersonal violence. However, this study has demonstrated that cruelty committed against animals often reveals insightful analogies with violence against humans by humans.

Past acts of cruelty to animals resembling either the subjects' instant or most serious offense were identified in some cases involving violent offenders. One violent subject, a repeat sex offender, had been convicted while an adolescent of a crime against nature for sodomizing a reformatory pig. Another subject, convicted of sexual battery on a person sixty-five years or older, described how he would throw stones and bricks at stray animals "to beat and hurt them like my parents hurt me." According to the police report, the victim's face had been severely beaten. One can only speculate whether these earlier incidents could have provided clues to a troubled youth who might not have subsequently hurt human beings had appropriate intervention and treatment occurred upon discovery of the animal cruelty.

Cruelty to animals, in and of itself, is not a definitive predictor of violence against humans. The reasons that humans commit acts of cruelty to animals indicate as much about human culture as they do about human violence. Boys who shoot birds with BB guns while playing war games may grow up to be soldiers—they may even someday kill other soldiers in a real war—but they may or may not become murderers. This study has demonstrated that the phenomenon of cruelty to animals must be examined within cultural contexts and within the parameters of cultural norms.

It has also demonstrated that acts of cruelty to animals that are committed in a deliberate and particularly brutal fashion can reveal behavior and motives that clearly signal danger with respect to future interpersonal violence. Furthermore, acts of cruelty to animals that violate the collective values and sensitivities of a society, such as stomping to death a puppy, are alarming. They clearly violate the social and behavioral norms and the cohesive, reciprocal bond of civility that a humane society requires for its very survival.

The results of this study indicate that cruelty to animals committed by children can provide insights into violent behavior that may or may not translate into later violence directed against humans. Therefore, cruelty to animals must be investigated in terms of its complex dynamics if useful and meaningful insight is to be extrapolated. The type of cruelty committed, the type of animal targeted, the motivation for the cruelty, and the perpetrator's response to the cruelty are critical factors that must be considered.

To dismiss cruelty to animals as incidental acts committed by troubled kids is to dismiss an opportunity to identify behavior that might indeed be a precursor of violence against humans. Our findings strongly suggest that each act of cruelty to animals, which is but one expression of violence, should be investigated with rigorous attentions to the specifics involved. Every act should be investigated as a specific act committed by a specific individual committed against a specific animal. It would appear that by implementing this approach, acts of cruelty to animals that are relevant to the relationship of cruelty to animals and later violence against humans might be distinguished from those that are not.

Clearly, the phenomenon of violence is as complicated as its sources, the physiology and psychology of human beings. At this point it is not known to what extent violence is the product of nature or nurture, or both interactively. Its manifestations, however, often appear to be as unique as the individuals who commit it. Likewise, the reasons that many individuals avoid violence are highly individualized. Both violence and avoidance of violence must be examined systematically to detect patterns, to intervene early, and to prevent violence.

Procedures and methods to prevent violence, like criminal profiling, are not an exact science. Violence prevention requires both objectivity and a subjective empathy toward both humans and animals. Cruelty to animals leaves many victims. It causes animals to suffer and deprives them of their lives. It often causes humans great psychological pain because they have been deprived of the animals they loved. Finally, cruelty to animals causes society to suffer because it deprives society of its very humanity and goodness. Perhaps this result is what Mead meant when she emphasized the danger to society that cruelty to "good" animals engenders. If the study of cruelty to animals can ultimately help save lives, be they human or animal, then it is both a practical and an ethical endeavor.

Recommendations for Future Research

Cruelty to animals is undoubtedly a complex phenomenon whose understanding requires precise conceptual and descriptive analysis. A continued refinement of the methodologies applied to the study of cruelty to animals will facilitate further research and result in a more meaningful and useful understanding of the phenomenon. The concepts and definitions applied must take into account humans' often contradictory perceptions of animals. These perceptions are both individually and culturally determined, and they directly influence the treatment of animals in any given society.

Forms of Animal Cruelty

To facilitate greater understanding of the concept of animal cruelty, we propose definitions of seven forms of animal cruelty. These definitions, although not mutually exclusive, establish distinct conceptual parameters by which to more clearly articulate cruelty in its many manifestations.

1. *Passive cruelty*: the observation of a cruel act in which the observer neither participates nor intervenes (e.g., an adolescent observes other adolescents setting fire to a cat).

2. *Participatory cruelty*: the active participation by one or more individuals in a cruel act (e.g., three individuals act cooperatively to pour gasoline onto a stray cat and to set it on fire).

3. *Perfunctory cruelty*: a cruel act most often committed by a child either alone or with same-age peers in which the targeted animal(s) is perceived to be a literal target, inanimate and devoid of sentience. (Subjects who had engaged in this type of cruelty most often described the respective animals as targets. The acts themselves were often described as "war games" or "childish pastimes." In many instances, subjects who had committed such acts later expressed remorse that they had so casually and unthinkingly committed them, and recognized the acts to be inherently cruel.)

4. *Parochial cruelty*: animal cruelty that is regionally or culturally generated. These acts are often not considered cruel by the participants (e.g., dogfights, cockfights).

5. *Partitive cruelty*: animal cruelty that results from conceptual compartmentalizations applied to animals. This type of cruelty reduces animals to convenient labels and legitimizes cruelty by implementing arbitrary paradigms (e.g., the same individual may categorize animals in these ways: dog = pet; cow = food; squirrel = pest; bird = target; cat = plaything).

6. *Psychological cruelty*: animal cruelty that results from the particularities and peculiarities of the human mind and its conscious, subconscious, unconscious, psychic, cognitive, intellectual,

emotional, and/or pathological manifestations. *Phobic cruelty* is a form of psychological cruelty that results from the abuser's irrational fear of the animal. For example, ophidiophobia, the fear of snakes, appears to be common within the generalized human population.

7. *Predatory cruelty*: animal cruelty that is purposeful, planned, and often sequential in execution. [This type of cruelty is exemplified by the subject who went into the woods and spear-hunted wild animals and stray dogs with the express goal of killing for its own sake. This goal differs from the goals associated with legitimate hunting, the acquisition of meat (food) and/or a trophy (sport).]

As noted, these forms of cruelty are not mutually exclusive. Rather, these definitions are intended to broaden understanding by providing meaningful categories that can be further studied and possibly used to chart appropriate interventions and serve as warning signals. For example, the spear-hunter cited with respect to predatory cruelty can also be cited with respect to psychological cruelty. In keeping with the Displaced Aggression Theory proposed in this work, the predatory behavior that the subject exhibited toward the animals he hunted appeared psychologically motivated. Ultimately, the psychological anger that the subject experienced internally was externalized and displaced against the animals, and later the humans, that he targeted. In the proposed framework, animal cruelty of this type might have signaled the need for immediate in-depth psychological treatment to resolve apparent internal conflict.

Parental Abuse and Family Dysfunction

Parental abuse and familial dysfunction appeared to be key factors in the development of aggressive and/or dysfunctional tendencies in most of the subjects studied. The study demonstrated that both nonviolent and violent subjects were frequently victims of parental abuse and familial dysfunction. The data suggested that the subjects' *perceptions of* and *reactions to* the abuse and dysfunction that they encountered appeared to be important discriminating factors when violent and nonviolent subjects were compared. Obviously, this assumption is qualitatively drawn and was not statistically measured. The study did reveal that those subjects who had expressed empathy for their own unfortunate circumstances and for others affected by the abuse, such as a mother or sibling, had committed violent crimes less frequently. The role of empathy as a protective factor in reducing violent behavior among those who have been abused, who have witnessed cruelty to animals or humans, or who have mistreated animals clearly warrants systematic investigation.

This study provided support for the proposition that criminal and violent behavior are indeed two distinct behaviors, as argued more than thirty years ago by Climent, Hyg, and Erwin (1972). Undoubtedly, many of the nonviolent subjects studied were tied to a criminal lifestyle that was long-standing and pervasive. However, violence had not been a part of that history. Furthermore, many of the nonviolent subjects had endured extreme parental abuse. Although the abuse and dysfunction that shaped the personalities and psyches of these subjects might well have been significant factors in determining their criminality, violence was not a component of that criminality. Further research should be conducted in an effort to better understand *criminal* behavior as distinct from *violent* behavior. Future studies should attempt to identify the factors that distinguish nonviolent criminality from violent criminality and that are operative in inhibiting aggressive tendencies

Cruelty to animals can be a viable indicator not only of individuals at risk of committing violence but also of individuals who are at risk of having violence committed against them. A number of the subjects in this study observed acts of cruelty committed by parental figures against animals they loved. The cruelty to animals that they observed was also cruelty committed against them in the form of psychological abuse. If the cruelty had come to the attention of a teacher or other professional, perhaps appropriate intervention might have been orchestrated.

Child abuse, like spouse abuse, is insidious and often cloaked in secrecy. However, most children are responsive to caring adults, and most have a natural fondness for, and curiosity about, animals. Humane education can be an effective tool to identify children and animals at risk. Humane education teaches children that both animals and children deserve and require the protection, respect, and love of responsible and compassionate adults. Within this context, abused children can make the connection to their own abuse and, in a trusting environment, might reach out for help. Conversely, the behavior of children who show no empathy for animals and have committed cruelty to animals should be monitored and rigorously documented in applicable case files, such as school and court files. Understandably, issues of confidentiality factor into this process, particularly where juveniles are concerned. Indeed, such issues are presently being addressed in many courts around the country.

Cruelty to animals committed by children should be viewed as a serious and alarming offense that requires intervention. This view should be shared by all concerned, including law enforcement officers, educators, health and family service providers, animal welfare officials, and judges. These institutions should make a cooperative effort to develop an integrated database system to track and share information about cruelty to animals. Animal control officers and animal cruelty investigators are valuable resources for this effort and should be consulted to facilitate this process. Working together, these individuals and the institutions they represent can more effectively address cruelty to animals and proactively intervene on behalf of the many victims, both animal and human, that such cruelty leaves in its wake. Indeed, much of the literature to date expresses the common theme that various elements of society must join cooperatively to effectively address the issue of cruelty to animals (see, e.g., Arluke et al., 1999; Crowell, 1999; Ascione, 2000; Lewchanin & Zimmerman, 2000; Ponder & Lockwood, 2000; Turner, 2000; Flynn, 2001).

Conclusions

Clearly, cruelty to animals is a complicated phenomenon that requires continued research. However, it also appears clear from the research to date that cruelty to animals is not an abstraction, devoid of human connection, that affects merely its animal victims. Rather, compelling evidence has been offered by a significant number of studies to indicate that cruelty to animals is indeed tied to the affairs and interactions of humans who operate in the complex arena we define as culture. In this respect, Margaret Mead's prophetic warning that "one of the most dangerous things that can happen to a child is to kill or torture an animal and get away with it" (Lockwood & Hodge, 1998) bears repeating. Ultimately, the phenomenon of cruelty to animals must be addressed on various levels in view of the many ways that animals interact with humans. As Cazaux

(1999) suggested, it may now be time to address cruelty to animals within a nonspeciesist context rather than from the traditional anthropocentric viewpoint that has historically driven both investigation and intervention with respect to cruelty to animals. In closing, we concur with the challenge posed by Clifton Flynn: "if we are to promote a nonviolent society, then we must pay attention to all forms of violence, including violence against animals" (Flynn, 2000, p. 94).

AFTERWORD:
TOM NERO, MARY BELL, AND ADVANCES IN
THE STUDY OF ANIMAL ABUSE

Tom Nero's life did not have an auspicious beginning. Residing in a welfare facility for abandoned, orphaned, or destitute children, he often roamed the streets of his city seeking diversions with his youthful peers. Pitiably, the abuse and torture of animals were common forms of whiling away an otherwise boring, aimless, and, perhaps, impotent existence. Tom and his peers were terribly creative in the forms of physical maltreatment they inflicted on the defenseless animals in their midst, and sexual assaults on animals occurred as well.

Tom entered adolescence employed yet still tainted by his propensity to abuse and maltreat those under his control. A "disobedient" horse, unable to meet Tom's demands because it had a broken leg, was beaten mercilessly, one of its eyes gouged during the assault. His childhood abuse of animals had metamorphosed into even more vicious cruelties.

Tempted by the lure of more readily obtained riches, Tom, now a young adult, turned to a life of crime. Thefts, sometimes committed with a firearm, were clearly less labor intensive and more lucrative than honest employment and became his primary means of "earning" an income. Unsatisfied with the booty from his own criminal activities, Tom tried to coerce his girlfriend to steal from her employer. In anger over her reluctance, Tom slit her throat, killing her and the unborn child with whom she was pregnant. Tom was apprehended, tried, convicted of murder, and executed.

An elaboration on one of the case studies included in this timely, meticulously researched, and thought-provoking study by Linda Merz-Perez and Kathleen Heide? No—Tom Nero was the fictional creation of the British artist William Hogarth, who used his creative skills to call attention to animal welfare in the mid-1700s (Shesgreen, 1973), decades before the establishment of the Royal SPCA. His engraving *The Four*

Stages of Cruelty outlined the potential progression from childhood and adolescent animal abuse to adult interpersonal violence, a progression alluded to by philosophers who predated Hogarth, like John Locke, and by current mental health professionals. Merz-Perez and Heide have addressed an issue that has perplexed us for centuries. Is there a relation between our treatment of nonhuman animals and the way we treat our fellow human beings? And if such a relation exists, how do we account for it? These questions are not posed to satisfy idle curiosity. The answers to the questions are valuable to all who care about the welfare of society and the mental health and safety of its individual members.

This study is also embedded within a historical period when an increasing number of states have added felony-level animal abuse statutes to their criminal codes. This change reflects the increasing seriousness with which law enforcement and the judiciary view cases of egregious animal abuse. In addition, it indicates that animal abuse is being regarded as potentially criminal behavior even when "graduation" to violence against humans has not been demonstrated. Many states have also included provisions for the psychological evaluation of, and therapy for, individuals convicted of felony-level animal abuse. Efforts at evaluation and therapy cry out for a better understanding of the forms that cruelty to animals may take and the varied motivations that underlie such cruelty. In this regard, Merz-Perez and Heide's work provides an analysis rich in potential contributions to these assessment and therapeutic endeavors.

The authors offer an excellent overview of the history of animal welfare in England and the United States and enlighten the reader with comprehensive and up-to-date coverage of previously published integrative reviews of this topic, many of which have only appeared within the past decade. Merz-Perez and Heide have conducted a comprehensive research project in the tradition of Alan Felthous and his colleagues' pioneering studies of the relations among animal cruelty, criminal and violent behavior (see Lockwood & Ascione, 1998), and mental health. The timeliness of Merz-Perez and Heide's work is also illustrated by a recently published paper by Gleyzer, Felthous, and Holzer (2002) in which violent criminals with a history of substantial animal abuse were found to be more likely than criminals without this history to fit the diagnostic characteristics of antisocial personality disorder. Using more refined and detailed assessments than in past research, Merz-Perez and Heide have reexamined the animal abuse histories of significant numbers of incarcerated men and have explored the developmental histories of these perpetrators to glean clues about personal and familial factors that differentiate those who abuse animals from those who do not, or at least not to the same degree. As noted by the respected authority on violence James Gilligan, "The lessons we learn from the prison population can turn out to be helpful and even necessary if we want to be able to learn how to help people in the community who are not (yet) so damaged" (Gilligan, 2001, p. 121).

This project was no small undertaking. Respectful of the rights of the imprisoned, Merz-Perez and Heide made certain that securing informed consent, implementing high ethical standards related to confidentiality and sensitivity to the mental health needs of participants, and conforming to institutional research protocols were each given high priority. Aside from meeting these cumbersome yet critically important research standards, the authors embarked on the perhaps even more challenging approach of individually interviewing each of their participants. The fruits of these labors are evident in the quantitative analyses presented in this book but even more so in the rich qualitative information gleaned from the countless hours of listening to the stories of men whose potentially productive lives were derailed and whose behavior has negatively affected many of the humans and animals who have crossed their criminal and violent paths.

The work of these authors also illustrates the evolution of the scientific study of animal abuse or cruelty to animals. Decades ago, it was sufficient to ask, "Has this person been cruel to animals?" with little attention to defining either "cruelty" or "animals." Merz-Perez and Heide, aware of the deficits of ambiguous questioning and respondents' ambiguous answers, have approached assessment with detailed questions about their participants' experiences with animals based, in part, on an assessment approach Teresa Thompson, Tracy Black, and I developed a number of years ago entitled the Cruelty to Animals Assessment Instrument (CAAI) (Ascione, Thompson, & Black, 1997). Although the CAAI was originally developed for use with children, adolescents, and their parents or caretakers, Merz-Perez and Heide adapted it for use with their adult criminal sample in what I believe is the first independently published study using the CAAI. It is very encouraging that the numerical scores derived from the CAAI clearly differentiated the violent and nonviolent criminals in their sample and that surveying participants' experiences with a number of types of animals (pet, stray, farm, and wild) also yielded valuable information and questions for future research. A recently published study by Guymer, Mellor, Luk, and Pearse (2001) also demonstrated that a checklist assessment, also based on the CAAI but easier to administer and score, was useful in examining the animal abuse history of conduct disordered children.

Yes, animal abuse varies in frequency, severity, the types of animals abused, and myriad other variables. Merz-Perez and Heide examine these variables but also include attention to the motivations that may underlie animal abuse, the sociocultural factors that may influence our judgments of the perpetrator's culpability, and developmental factors that may have contributed to the emergence and maintenance of violent behavior. Recall the character Lenny Small in Steinbeck's (1937/1992) *Of Mice and Men.* Mentally challenged, Lenny could not distinguish nurturing touch from destructive embraces, and both animals and humans fell victim to this deficit. In the case of Mary Bell, an eleven-year-old who strangled two preschool boys to death in England and who was also known for her cruelty to animals (Sereny, 1972, 1998), examination of her infancy and childhood experiences of emotional, physical, and sexual abuse shed light on what factors might create a child so young yet capable of such horrific interpersonal violence. A violent, murderous child? Yes. A history of animal abuse? Yes. Behavior legally categorized as criminal? Certainly. An eleven-year-old culpable for her acts? Here, the answer is less certain. To paraphrase the words of Andrew Vachss, "We [caretakers] are tested, and sometimes we fail. The maltreated child cries, 'I hurt.' Unheard or unheeded, that cry (may) become prophecy" (1993, p. 21).

The authors also observe that animal abuse may be compartmentalized (e.g., the person who is "retaliating" against a particular animal but has no animosity toward other animals) further complicating our understanding of this phenomenon. Merz-Perez and Heide interviewed men whose caring for their dogs seems anomalous given that they entered these same animals in potentially lethal dogfights. Culture is both a lens through which the perpetrator interprets his acts and a lens the researcher must use to qualify the meaning and intent of animal abuse. And the reader is struck by the number of men who shared their experiences of witnessing violence toward animals perpetrated by adults who played a caretaking role (one participant's recollection of being forced to watch his dog consume food his father had purposely laced with broken glass is a vivid example). The effect of a child's *witnessing* animal abuse cannot be dismissed as insignificant in the development or erosion of empathy in that child's life. In cases where the abused animal was loved by the child, we might ask how attachments to the abusing caretaker(s) were distorted by these displays of violence and cruelty. But there are also examples of healing scattered throughout this study. One nonviolent criminal who, as a child, killed a neighbor's pig with a gun given to him by his grandfather apparently learned a lesson in restorative justice. His grandfather broke the gun and required that his grandson help the neighbor care for the remaining pigs.

In reflecting on their work, these authors acknowledge that animal abuse is likely multifaceted and may emerge from, and be determined by, a variety of different backgrounds. Their call for the formation of coalitions, agency collaborations, and multidisciplinary scholarly approaches to the problem is timely and one I wholeheartedly endorse. So too is their encouragement of a central data collection system to record, nationally, the incidence of this obviously significant form of violence against living creatures. Recall our ability to ignore the problem of child maltreatment in our nation until yearly statistics shook us out of our complacency. In this vein, a series of recent papers have begun to quantify the scope of animal abuse encountered by veterinarians in their clinical practice (Munro, 1996; Munro & Thrushfield, 2001a,b, c, and d).

As with any thoughtful and creative research endeavor, the study reported by Merz-Perez and Heide raises new questions and prompts revisiting old questions with more refined and contemporary methodologies. First, this study is a laudable example of retrospective approaches to understanding a phenomenon. Retrospective studies, which rely on the participants' recollection of events, experiences, and behaviors in their past, is a common strategy, allowing for the rapid and efficient collection of potentially large amounts of historical information. Although subject to selective recall, memory decay, and intentional and unintentional biases in reporting, it remains a popular method of data gathering. The value of the information gathered by Merz-Perez and Heide will become even more evident if their study prompts longitudinal, prospective research to examine the varied courses that animal abuse may take when it emerges in childhood (Ascione, 2003, in press). For example, retrospective research with adults who abuse children suggests that significant majorities of these individuals were themselves victimized as children. Yet prospective research with victims of child maltreatment indicates that a much smaller percentage become abusive adults. What forms of childhood animal abuse predict later interpersonal violence? Does the manner in which caretakers respond to animal abuse by their children affect desistence or maintenance and escalation? How is the development (or lack thereof) of empathy involved in the course of cruel and abusive behavior? I am certain that Merz-Perez and Heide would agree that our best prospect for minimizing animal abuse is early intervention, and answers to these questions will be immensely helpful in this endeavor.

Second, Merz-Perez and Heide are to be commended for the comprehensive nature of the assessments they conducted, that is, including both "Ascione" animal abuse variables and "Heide" human abuse and family functioning variables. And yet, here lie both a strength and a weakness inherent in their strategy. The level of detailed information gathered in this project is unparalleled in previous studies in this area. But the labor-intensive nature of this process limited, understandably, the number of participants who could be included. With a larger sample of participants, interesting and important cross tabulations between the Ascione and Heide variables could have been examined. For example, is animal abuse more common among violent criminals who also have histories of severe abuse as children than for violent criminals without such histories? Is family dysfunction or substance abuse associated with animal abuse in children exposed to such compromised parenting? Questions such as these must await future work with even larger samples that will allow for the creation of subgroups with sufficient numbers of participants.

Third, there is a need to consider the role of biological factors in predisposing some to violent and abusive behavior. For example, the severe abuse histories of some of the participants in this study suggest that head injuries may not have been uncommon. Dorothy Lewis (1998) and Jonathon Pincus (2001), in their work with violent youths and adults, have made a compelling case that injuries to the head may affect brain development, functioning, and organization important to the development of inhibitory controls and appropriate empathic responding. This issue may be especially relevant to the study of animal abuse in violent, incarcerated individuals since animal victims may be so similar to human victims in their vulnerability, ability to express pain and distress, and to succumb to the effects of abuse and violent attacks (Ascione & Arkow, 1999). The authors' findings on differences in empathy between violent and nonviolent criminals highlight the importance of this issue and a need for further exploration of the development of empathy.

Finally, although the authors allude to a few cases of bestiality reported by their participants, the significance of this form of animal abuse should be given greater attention. The domination of a helpless animal coupled with the perpetrator's sexual arousal and with injuries to, or the death of, the animal sexually assaulted is a terrible recipe for deviant sexual arousal. Given the social undesirability of bestiality, even among criminal samples, it may be that we underestimate the prevalence of sexual assaults on animals. Future studies should examine this phenomenon in greater detail.

Our understanding of the phenomenon of animal abuse has been advanced significantly by Merz-Perez and Heide's efforts. Their work should attract the attention of students and professionals who work in the fields of psychology, psychiatry, law, criminology, social work, child welfare, and family violence. The interested layperson will also benefit from this book since it presents a thoughtful and concise overview of animal abuse and the characteristics of those who perpetrate it. The book will no doubt become a classic reference in this field, one whose fruits will be even more sophisticated and probing studies of this form of violence and abuse. Healing often begins with a journey of understanding. Merz-Perez and Heide have hastened our travel along this path.

—Frank R. Ascione, Ph.D.

REFERENCES

Achenbach, T. M., Howell, C. T., Quay, H. C., & Connors, C. K.
1991. National survey of problems and competencies among four- to sixteen-year-olds. *Monographs of the Society for Research in Child Development*, 56: Serial No. 255.

Agnew, R.
1998. The causes of animal abuse: A social-psychological analysis. *Theoretical Criminology*, 2, 177–209.

American Psychiatric Association.
1994. *Diagnostic and statistical manual of mental disorders* (4th ed.). Washington, DC: American Psychiatric Association.

Arkow, P.
1996. The relationships between animal abuse and other forms of family violence. *Family and Sexual Assault Bulletin*, 12, 29–34.

———.

1998. The correlations between cruelty to animals and child abuse and the implications for veterinary medicine. In R. Lockwood and F. R. Ascione (eds.), *Cruelty to animals and interpersonal violence* (pp. 409–414). West Lafayette, IN: Purdue University Press.

Arluke, A., Levin, J., Luke, C., and Ascione, F. R.
1999. The relationship of animal abuse to violence and other forms of antisocial behavior. *Journal of Interpersonal Violence*, 14, 963–975.

Arluke, A., and Lockwood, R.
1997. Guest editor's introduction: Understanding cruelty to animals. *Society and Animals*, 5, 183–193.

REFERENCES

Ascione, F. R.
1993. Children who are cruel to animals: A review of research and implications for developmental psychopathology. *Anthrozoös*, 6, 226–247.

———.
1997. Nature and status of research on the link between animal cruelty and child abuse. *Protecting Children*, 13 (2), 12–14.

———.
1998a. Battered women's reports of their partners' and their children's cruelty to animals. *Journal of Emotional Abuse*, 1, 119–133.

———.
1998b. Children who are cruel to animals: A review of research and implications for developmental psychopathology. In R. Lockwood and F. R. Ascione (eds.), *Cruelty to animals and interpersonal violence* (pp. 83–104). West Lafayette, IN: Purdue University Press.

———.
1999. The abuse of animals and human interpersonal violence: Making the connection. In F. R. Ascione and P. Arkow (eds.), *Child abuse, domestic violence, and animal abuse: Linking the circles of compassion for prevention and intervention* (pp. 50–61). West Lafayette, IN: Purdue University Press.

———.
2001, September. Animal abuse and youth violence. *Juvenile Justice Bulletin*, 1–15.

———.
2003, in press. *Children and animals, kindness and cruelty.* New York: Oxford University Press.

Ascione, F. R., & Arkow, P.
1999. *Child abuse, domestic violence, and animal abuse: Linking the circles of compassion for prevention and intervention.* West Lafayette, IN: Purdue University Press.

Ascione, F. R., and Lockwood, R.
2001. Cruelty to animals: Changing psychological, social, and legislative perspectives. In D. J. Salem and A. N. Rowan (eds.), *State of the animals 2000* (pp. 39–53). Washington, DC: Humane Society Press.

Ascione, F. R., Thompson, T. M., & Black, T.
1997. Childhood cruelty to animals: Assessing cruelty dimensions and motivations. *Anthrozoös*, 10 (4), 170–179.

Baumann, E.
1991. *Step into my parlor.* Chicago: Bonus Books.

Beirne, P.
1997. Rethinking bestiality: Towards a sociology of interspecies sexual assault. *Theoretical Criminology,* 1, 317–340.

Bender, L.
1959. Children and adolescents who have killed. *American Journal of Psychiatry,* 116, 510–513.

Billitteri, T. J.
1993, June 19. Santeria ruling hailed as victory. *The St. Petersburg Times,* pp. E1, E4.

Bronfenbrenner, U., & Morris, P. A.
1997. The ecology of developmental processes. In W. Damon (ed.). *Handbook of Child Psychology,* 5th ed. New York: Wiley.

Cazaux, G.
1999. Beauty and the beast: Animal abuse from a non-speciesist criminological perspective. *Crime Law and Social Change,* 31, 105–126.

Climent, C. E., Hyg, R., & Erwin, F. R.
1972. Historical data in the evaluation of violent subjects. *Archives of General Psychiatry,* 27, 621–624.

Cox, M.
1991. *The confessions of Henry Lee Lucas.* New York: Pocket Star Books.

Crowell, S.
1999. Animal cruelty as it relates to child abuse: Shedding light on a "hidden" problem. *Journal of Juvenile Law,* 22, 38–59.

Davis, D.
1991. *Milwaukee murders.* New York: St. Martin's Press.

DeViney, E., Dickert, J., & Lockwood, R.
1983. The care of pets within abusing families. *International Journal of the Study of Animal Problems,* 4, 321–329.

Douglas, J., Burgess, A. W., Burgess, A. G., & Ressler, R. K.
1997. *Crime classification manual.* San Francisco: Jossey-Bass.

Douglas, J., & Olshaker, M.
1995. *Mindhunter: Inside the FBI's elite serial crime unit.* New York: Simon and Schuster.

REFERENCES

Duncan, A., & Miller, C.
2002. The impact of an abusive family context on childhood animal cruelty and adult violence. *Aggression and Violent Behavior,* 7, 365–383.

Dvorchak, R. J., & Holewa, L.
1991. *Milwaukee massacre.* New York: Dell.

Dwyer, K., Osher, D., & Warger, C.
1998. *Early warning, timely response: A guide to safe schools.* Washington, DC: U.S. Department of Education.

Easson, W. M., & Steinhilber, R. M.
1961. Murderous aggression by children and adolescents. *Archives of General Psychiatry,* 4, 1–9.

Favre, D., & Tsang, V.
1993. The development of anti-cruelty laws during the 1800s. *Detroit College of Law Review,* 1, 1–35.

——.
1997. The development of anti-cruelty laws during the 1800s. In R. Lockwood & F. R. Ascione (eds.), *Cruelty to animals and interpersonal violence* (pp. 32–66). West Lafayette, IN: Purdue University Press.

Felthous, A. R., & Kellert, S. R.
1987. Childhood cruelty to animals and later aggression against people: A review. *American Journal of Psychiatry,* 144, 710–717.

Flynn, C. P.
1999. Animal abuse in childhood and later support for interpersonal violence in families. *Society and Animals,* 7, 161–172.

——.
2000. Why family professionals can no longer ignore violence toward animals. *Family Relations,* 49 (1), 87–95.

Gerome, J.
1999, January 28. Ruler of the roosts. *The Birmingham News,* pp. E1, E3.

Gilligan, J.
2001. *Preventing violence.* New York: Thames and Hudson.

Gleyzer, R., Felthous, A. R., & Holzer III, C. E.
2002. Animal cruelty and psychiatric disorders. *Journal of the American Academy of Psychiatry and the Law,* 30 (2), 257–265.

Grandin, T.
1988. Behavior of slaughter plant and auction employees toward the animals. *Anthrozoös*, 1, 205–213.

Guymer, E. C., Mellor, D., Luk, E. S. L., & Pearse, V.
2001. The development of a screening questionnaire for childhood cruelty to animals. *Journal of Child Psychology and Psychiatry*, 42 (8), 1057–1063.

Heide, K. M.
1992. *Why kids kill parents*. Columbus: Ohio State University Press.

———.
1999. *Young killers*. Thousand Oaks, CA: Sage Publications.

Hellman, D. S., & Blackman, N.
1966. Enuresis, firesetting, and cruelty to animals: A triad predictive of adult crime. *American Journal of Psychiatry*, 122, 1431–1435.

Hickey, E. W.
2002. *Serial murderers and their victims*. Belmont, CA: Wadsworth/Thomson Learning.

Holmes, R. M., & Holmes, S. T.
1996. *Profiling violent crimes*. Newberry Park, CA: Sage Publications.

Holmes, R. M., & De Burger, J.
1988. *Serial murder*. Newbury Park, CA: Sage Publications.

Justice, E., Justice R., & Kraft, I. A.
1974. Early warning signs of violence: Is the triad enough? *American Journal of Psychiatry*, 131, 457–459.

Kellert, S. R., & Felthous, A. R.
1985. Childhood cruelty toward animals among criminals and noncriminals. *Human Relations*, 38, 1113–1129.

Keeney, B. T., & Heide, K. M.
1993. The latest on serial murderers. *Violence Update*, 4, 1–2, 4, 10.

———.
1995. Serial murder: A more accurate and inclusive definition. *International Journal of Offender Therapy and Comparative Criminology*, 39 (4), 299–306.

Lane, S.
1997. Assessment of sexually abusive youth. In G. Ryan & S. Lane (eds.), *Juvenile sexual offending: Causes, consequences, and correction* (pp. 219–263). San Francisco: Jossey-Bass.

Lewchanin, S., & Zimmerman, E.
2000. *Clinical assessment of juvenile animal cruelty.* Brunswick, ME: Biddle Publishing.

Lewis, D. O.
1998. *Guilty by reason of insanity: A psychiatrist explores the minds of killers.* New York: Fawcett Columbine.

Lewis, D. O., Shanok, S. S., Grant, M., & Ritvo, E.
1983. Homicidally aggressive young children: Neuro-psychiatric and experimental correlates. *American Journal of Psychiatry,* 140, 148–153.

Lifton, R. J.
1986. *The Nazi doctors: Medical killing and the psychology of genocide.* New York: Basic Books.

Lockwood, R.
1999. Animal cruelty and societal violence: A brief look back from the front. In F. R. Ascione & P. Arkow (eds.), *Child abuse, domestic violence, and animal abuse* (pp. 3–8). West Lafayette, IN: Purdue University Press.

Lockwood, R., & Ascione, F. R. (eds.).
1998. *Cruelty to animals and interpersonal violence: Readings in research and application.* West Lafayette, IN: Purdue University Press.

Lockwood, R., & Church, A.
1998. Deadly serious: An FBI perspective on animal cruelty. In R. Lockwood & F. A. Ascione (eds.), *Cruelty to animals and interpersonal violence* (pp. 241–246). West Lafayette, IN: Purdue University Press.

Lockwood, R. & Hodge, G. R.
1998. The tangled web of animal abuse: The links between cruelty to animals and human violence. In R. Lockwood and F. R. Ascione (eds.), *Cruelty to animals and interpersonal violence* (pp. 77–82). West Lafayette, IN: Purdue University Press.

Loeber, R., Farrington, D. P., & Waschbusch, D. A.
1998. Serious and violent juvenile offenders. In R. Loeber & D. P. Farrington (eds.), *Serious and violent juvenile offenders: Risk factors and successful interventions* (pp. 13–29). Thousand Oaks, CA: Sage Publications.

Luk, E. S. L., Staiger, P. K., Wong, L., & Mathai, J.
1999. Children who are cruel to animals: A revisit. *Australian and New Zealand Journal of Psychiatry,* 33, 29–36.

MacDonald, J. M.
1963. The threat to kill. *American Journal of Psychiatry*, 8, 125–130.

Mason, J., & Singer, P.
1990. *Animal factories*. New York: Harmony Books.

Mead, M.
1964. Cultural factors in the cause and prevention of pathological homicide. *The Bulletin of the Menninger Clinic*, 28, 11–22.

Miller, C.
2001. Childhood animal cruelty and interpersonal violence. *Clinical Psychology Review*, 21, 735–749.

Miller, K. S., & Knutson, J. F.
1997. Reports of severe physical punishment and exposure to animal cruelty by inmates convicted of felonies and by university students. *Child Abuse and Neglect*, 21, 59–82.

Munro, H.
1996. "Battered pets." *Irish Veterinary Journal*, 49, 712–713.

Munro, H., & Thrushfield, M. V.
2001a. Battered pets: Features that raise suspicion of non-accidental injury. *Journal of Small Animal Practice*, 42, 218–226.

———.

2001b. Battered pets: Non-accidental physical injuries found in dogs and cats. *Journal of Small Animal Practice*, 42, 279–290.

———.

2001c. Battered pets: Sexual abuse. *Journal of Small Animal Practice*, 42, 333–337.

———.

2001d. Battered pets: Munchausen syndrome by proxy (fictitious illness by proxy). *Journal of Small Animal Practice*, 42, 385–389.

Norris, J.
1988. *Serial killers*. New York: Doubleday.

Osgood, D. W., Johnston, L. D., O'Malley, P. M., & Bachman, J. G.
1988. The generality of deviance in late adolescence and early adulthood. *American Sociological Review*, 53, 81–93.

Owens, D. J., & Straus, M. A.
1975. The social structure of violence in childhood and approval of violence as an adult. *Aggressive Behavior,* 1, 193–211.

Pincus, J. H.
2001. *Base instincts: What makes killers kill.* New York: W. W. Norton.

Ponder, C., & Lockwood, R.
2000. Programs educate law enforcement on link between animal cruelty and domestic violence. *The Police Chief,* 67, 31–36.

Quinlisk, A.
1995. Domestic violence intervention survey project. Unpublished paper. Lacrosse, WI.

Quinlisk, J. A.
1999. Animal abuse and family violence. In F. R. Ascione & P. Arkow (eds.), *Child abuse, domestic violence, and animal abuse* (pp. 168–175). West Lafayette, IN: Purdue University Press.

Raschke, C. A.
1990. *Painted black.* New York: HarperCollins.

Ressler, R. K., Burgess, A. W., Hartman, C. R., Douglas, J. E., & McCormack, A.
1998. Murderers who rape and mutilate. In R. Lockwood & F. R. Ascione (eds.), *Cruelty to animals and interpersonal violence* (pp. 179–193). West Lafayette, IN: Purdue University Press.

Reynolds, C. R. & Kamphaus, R. W.
1992. *Behavior assessment system for children: Teacher rating scales.* Circle Pines, MN: American Guidance Service.

Sakheim, G. A., & Osborne, E.
1994. *Firesetting children: Risk assessment and treatment.* Washington, DC: Child Welfare League of America.

Santtila, P., & Haapasalo, J.
1997. Neurological and psychological risk factors among young homicidal, violent, and nonviolent offenders in Finland. *Homicide Studies, 1*(3), 234–253.

Satten, J., Menninger, K., Rosen, I. & Mayman, M.
1960. Murder without apparent motive. *American Journal of Psychiatry,* 117, 48–53.

Schechter, H., & Everitt, D.
1996. *Encyclopedia of serial killers.* New York: Simon and Schuster.

Schiff, K., Louw, D., & Ascione, F. R.
1999. Animal relations in childhood and later violent behavior against humans. *Acta Criminologica*, 12, 77–86.

Schleuter, S.
1999. Animal abuse and law enforcement. In F. R. Ascione & Arkow, P. (eds.). *Child abuse, domestic violence, and animal abuse: Linking the circles of compassion for prevention and intervention.* (pp. 316–327). West Lafayette, IN: Purdue University Press.

Schwartz, A.
1992. *The man who could not kill enough.* New York: Carol Publishing Group.

Sendi, I. B., & Blomgren, P. G.
1975. A comparative study of predictive criteria in the predisposition of homicidal adolescents. *American Journal of Psychiatry*, 132, 423–427.

Sereny, G.
1972. *The case of Mary Bell.* New York: McGraw-Hill.

——.
1998. *Cries unheard: Why children kill—The story of Mary Bell.* New York: Henry Holt.

Shanok, S. S., Malani, S. C., Ninan, O. P., Guggenheim, P., Weinstein, H., & Otnow, D.
1983. A comparison of delinquent and nondelinquent adolescent psychiatric patients. *American Journal of Psychiatry*, 140, 582–585.

Shesgreen, S. (ed.)
1973. *Engravings by Hogarth.* New York: Dover Publications.

Spiegel, M.
1988. *The dreaded comparison: Human and animal slavery.* New York: Mirror Books.

Steinbeck, J.
1937/1992. *Of mice and men.* New York: Penguin Books.

Stone, R., & Kelner, K.
2000. Violence: No silver bullet. *Science*, 289, 569.

Tapia, F.
1971. Children who are cruel to animals. *Child Psychiatry and Human Development*, 2, 70–77.

Turner, N.
2000. Animal abuse and the link to domestic violence. *The Police Chief,* 67, 28–30.

Twitchell, J. B.
1989. *Preposterous violence: Fables of aggression in modern culture.* New York: Oxford University Press.

Vachss, A.
[1993]. *Another chance to get it right.* Milwaukie, OR: Dark Horse Publishing.

Vermeulen, H., & Odendaal, S. J.
1993. Proposed typology of companion animal abuse. *Anthrozoös,* 6, 248–257.

Wax, D. E., & Haddox, V. G.
1974a. Enuresis, fire setting, and animal cruelty: A useful danger signal in predicting vulnerability of adolescent males to assaultive behavior. *Child Psychiatry and Human Development,* 4, 151–156.

———.
1974b. Enuresis, firesetting, and animal cruelty in male adolescent delinquents: A triad predictive of violent behavior. *Journal of Psychiatry and Law,* 2, 245–271.

———.
1974c. Sexual aberrance in male adolescents manifesting a behavioral triad considered predictive of extreme violence: Some clinical observations. *Journal of Forensic Sciences,* 19, 102–108.

Wiegand, P., Schmidt, V., & Kleiber, M.
1999. German shepherd dog is suspected of sexually abusing a child. *International Journal of Legal Medicine,* 112, 324–325.

Wooden, W. S., & Berkey, M. L.
1984. *Children and arson: America's middle-class nightmare.* New York: Plenum Press.

Wright, J., & Hensley, C.
2003. From animal cruelty to serial murder: Applying the graduation hypothesis. *International Journal of Offender Therapy and Comparative Criminology,* 47 (1), 71–88.

Youssef, R. M., Attia, M. S., & Kamel, M. I.
1999. Violence among school children in Alexandria. *Eastern Mediterranean Health Journal,* 5, 282–298.

INDEX

cruelty to animals and later violence against humans, 151; test of the hypothesis, 90–93

Dahmer, J.: attempted creation of zombies to be sexual slaves, 62; example of Displaced Aggression Theory, 62–63; fascination with death, 62; killed by fellow inmate, 62; killed and impaled animals while still a juvenile, 49; rejection by parent, 62. *See also* foreword (p. ix)

Davis, D.: Dahmer longed to be noticed and accepted by parents, 62

De Burger, J., 57

DeSalvo, A.: acts of cruelty to animals committed by, 20; Boston Strangler, 20

DeViney, E.: abuse of pet animals, 42; animal abuse versus neglect, 42; behavior patterns toward animals in abusive families, 42; clearly defined criteria of cruel acts, 42

Diagnostic and Statistical Manual of Mental Disorders (*DSM-IV*), 28

Dickert, J., 42

Displaced Aggression Theory, 61–63; case study, 129–132

dogfighting, 94–96; as confounding variable, 95

domestic violence, 22

doubling, 46; as operative in the minds of humans with respect to their treatment of animals, 47–48

Douglas, J. E.: cruelty to animals and serial killers, 35; influence upon methodologies established by the FBI's Behavioral Sciences Unit, 34; profile of offender, 34; sexual

crime, 33; support for the significance of cruelty to animals as a predictor of future violence against humans, 33; triad, 34

Duncan, A.: effect of an abusive family context on childhood animal cruelty and adult violence, 45

Dvorchak, R. J.: Jeffrey Dahmer's attempted creation of zombies to be sexual slaves, 62

Dwyer, K.: importance of teachers' indirect observations with respect to animal cruelty, 28

Easson, W. M.: homicidal adolescent as the product of parental deprivation and dysfunction, 41

ecological theory, 33

empathy, 29; Ascione variable for, 82; lack of empathy as central factor in cruelty to animals, 29

enuresis, 6

Erwin, F. R., 38

Everitt, D., 20–21

family dynamics, 22; as examined by Kellert and Felthous, 22

farm animals, 98–99

Farrington, D. P., 27

Favre, D., 8

Federal Bureau of Investigation (FBI), 25

Federal Bureau of Investigation's Behavioral Sciences Unit, 29; cruelty to animals as viewed as important tool for identifying violent criminals, 29

Felthous, A. R.: acts of extreme cruelty to animals listed, 13; animal abuse and antisocial personality

ABOUT THE AUTHORS

Linda Merz-Perez has worked in the field of animal welfare for the past thirteen years. From 1990 to the present, she has served as a board member of the SPCA of West Pasco, Florida, and has held board positions with numerous other animal welfare organizations. From 1992 to 1998, she served as a court-appointed animal cruelty officer in Pasco County, Florida. She is a certified animal control officer and has received various awards for her work in the field, including the 1996 Justice Award, presented by the West Pasco Bar Association. From 1989 to 1998, she was an educator with Pinellas County schools, and from 1991 to 1995 she served as a guardian *ad litem* for the Sixth District Court, Florida. She holds an M.A. in criminology awarded in 1999 by the University of South Florida. From 1999 to 2002, she was the executive director of the Humane Society of Shelby County, Alabama. She currently serves on the boards of Hand-In-Paw and the Shelby Humane Society.

Kathleen M. Heide is professor of criminology at the University of South Florida, Tampa. She received her B.A. from Vassar College in psychology and her M.A. and Ph.D. in criminal justice from the State University of New York at Albany. She is an internationally recognized consultant on homicide and family violence. Her extensive publication record includes two widely acclaimed books on juvenile homicide, *Why Kids Kill Parents: Child Abuse and Adolescent Homicide* and *Young Killers: The Challenge of Juvenile Homicide*. She is a licensed psychotherapist and a court-appointed expert in matters relating to homicide, sexual battery, children, and families. Her work has been featured in popular magazines such as *Newsweek, U.S. News and World Report*, and *Psychology Today;* she has appeared as an expert on many nationally syndicated talk shows, including *Larry King Live, Geraldo, Sally Jesse Rafael,* and *Maury Povich.*

Randall Lockwood received a doctorate in psychology from Washington University in St. Louis and was on the faculty of the psychology departments of the State University of New York at Stony Brook and Washington University. He joined the staff of the Humane Society of the United States (HSUS) in 1984 and is currently vice president for research and educational outreach, overseeing professional education provided by the HSUS, the nation's largest animal protection organization. In his research, he has examined many different aspects of the interactions between people, animals, and nature, including the benefits of pet ownership to human health; the connection between cruelty to animals and other forms of violence; animal cruelty as a factor in the childhood of violent criminals; and the treatment of animals within child-abusing or otherwise disturbed families. His efforts with the HSUS to increase public and professional awareness of the connection between animal abuse and other forms of violence and to find creative approaches to the problems of violence in our society were profiled in an award-winning 1999 British Broadcast Corporation/Arts & Entertainment Network documentary entitled *The Cruelty Connection.* His book, *Cruelty to Animals and Interpersonal Violence,* coedited with Frank Ascione, was published in 1998. *Forensic Investigation of Animal Cruelty: A Guide for Veterinary and Law Enforcement Professionals,* coauthored with Leslie Sinclair, was published in 2003.

Frank R. Ascione received his bachelor's degree in psychology from Georgetown University in 1969 and his doctoral degree in developmental psychology from the University of North Carolina at Chapel Hill in 1973. He is a professor in the department of psychology and adjunct professor in family and human development at Utah State University. He has published a number of articles on the development of antisocial and pro-social behavior in children; coedited two books, *Cruelty to Animals and Interpersonal Violence: Readings in Research and Application* (1998), and *Child Abuse, Domestic Violence, and Animal Abuse: Linking the Circles of Compassion for Prevention and Intervention* (1998); and authored *Safe Havens for Pets: Guidelines for Programs Sheltering Pets for Women Who are Battered.* In the fall of 2001, the U.S. Office of Juvenile Justice and Delinquency Prevention published Ascione's review of animal abuse and youth violence as a research bulletin. He was selected to receive the 2001 Distinguished Scholar Award from the International Association of Human–Animal Interaction Organizations and the International Society for Anthrozoology. A member of the American Psychological Association and the Society for Research on Child Development, he serves on the Scientific Advisory Council of the Humane Society of the United States and the Child and Animal Abuse Prevention Advisory Council of the Latham Foundation. He is a member of the cadre of experts for the American Psychological Association's Presidential Task Force on Violence and the Family.

Printed in Great Britain
by Amazon